Healing the Victim

New Methods to Treat Victims of Life Abuses & Their Victimizers

EVALYN T. DUNDAS, Ph.D.

R&E Publishers • Saratoga, California

R & E Publishers
P.O. Box 2008, Saratoga, CA 95070
Tel: (408) 866-6303   Fax: (408) 866-0825

Book Design by Diane Parker
Cover by A.S.C.I.

Dundas, Evalyn.
    Healing the victim: new methods to treat victims of life abuses
    / Evalyn T. Dundas.
        p.   cm.
    Includes bibliographical references.
    ISBN 1-56875-080-3: $11.95
        1.   Victims--Mental health.   2. Psychotherapy.   3. Victims--Psychology. 4. Archetype (Psychology) I. Title.
    RC451.4.V53D86 1994
    616.89'17--dc20   94-1711
                                                       CIP

CONTENTS

I. VICTIM AS ARCHETYPE: A NEW APPROACH

The purpose of this book is to explore the archetypal meaning of victimization and its effects on our present culture. This study views victimization from the outer world of conscious events and from the inner world of unconscious imagery. It attempts to explore how a conscious connection to the Self (Higher Self) can heal both outer and inner wounds of the individual victim *caught* at the mercy of another person or by a continuing series of harsh events.

This theoretical study follows the author's own experience, research, and study of Jungian psychology. This approach does not overlook the importance of Freudian and more recent post-Freudian psychological theories. It does, however, consider first that there is a relationship between archetype and victimization, and that treatment often involves conscious sacrifice, or pain and submission, before the archetypes can be fully humanized and integrated.

This book explores how some victims are able to live the hero martyr role, while others are pulled into the passive role of inert victim. In the process, some history of child sacrifice and abuse, and a recognition of the forgotten inner child, is discussed. The book examines some of the deep victimizing influences that are erupting from the collective unconscious into our present culture. Further, it studies certain differences between the approach of analysts and psychoanalysts in understanding and treating trauma relative to victimization.

Despite today's increased awareness of child abuse and effective methods of treatment, many analysts and psychoanalysts pay insufficient attention to the archetypes that underlie victimization and to their implications for the healing process. In searching for deeper healing for victims and victimizers, we need to look more deeply into the complicated problems that underlie the recent epidemic of child abuse. One intention of the Jungian research described in this book is to clarify some of these problems. A glossary at the back of this book provides a clear definition of terms and Jungian terminology that may prove helpful to the reader.

Because of the orientation of this study, archetypal symbols are used as metaphors to provide deeper understanding of the inner experiences of both victim and victimizer. A clearer comprehension of the archetypes that underlie and influence the victim leads to a more effective treatment of the victim on all levels: child, adult, or family. The findings of this study will prove useful to clinicians who work with victims, as well as to patients who have been abused or victimized and can apply the material to their own specific experiences.

The Concept of Victimization and Archetype

The main hypothesis of this study is that the archetypal victim has been a part of the world from the beginning of creation. The archetypes representing both victim and victimizer are found in the collective unconscious. In other words there is still a collective archetypal image for good and for evil within each of us today. For example, all humanity shares the image of the self-sacrificing martyr as exemplified by early Christians who refused to renounce their belief in Christ and were put to death in many degrading and painful ways.

A distinction needs to be made between martyr and hero, or between passive and aggresive victim. In contrast to the self-sacrificing martyr, the hero martyr has found and knows his or her own center of power, allowing that individual to follow his or her own deep path. One example of the hero martyr is Laurens van der Post during his years in a Japanese prison camp in World War II, when he kept a large group of English soldiers strong in the face of very dreadful circumstances and terrible punishments by the Japanese guards.

Misused power is tragic, as seen in victim and bully archetypes, both in individual lives and in our mass victimization in society and in war situations. Too much self-sacrifice can destroy the ego, but when the hero victim speaks for humanity from a balanced inner connection to Self, both physical and psychic healing events can occur in the collective as well as the personal world.

Victimization implies suffering and submission to a higher order, but not a passive surrendering to painful circumstances. When an individual is born into a family that does not provide for the development of a strong ego, the individual is overwhelmed by physical or emotional difficulties. The individual's weak ego cannot withstand the onslaught of forces inside or outside the home that overpower his or her very center. The only choice for that individual in these circumstances is to identify with, or simply become, a self-sacrificing martyr—a victim.

It is essential for a victim who becomes possessed or overwhelmed by personal and collective suffering to *humanize*, the archetype that has made him or her powerless. A victim often projects an archetypal character, which is either *too perfect or too evil*, onto the human mother or father, or onto any close individual who may serve in an archetypal role. These archetypal projections must be made conscious before the person carrying the projection can be humanized and seen as an ordinary person.

Some Causes of Victimization

From the Jungian point of view, the victim becomes victimized after losing a sense of connection to the deep life forces. This simply means that when ego or psyche is overbalanced as *too good or too evil*, the individual has not integrated the opposites. For example, the individual may have put so much energy into work that he or she has no time for the family or for fun and joy. Symptoms of alienation are everywhere present in the modern world. Individuals seem to have lost the meaning of the deep spiritual symbols. An answer to "Who am I?" needs to come from the inside.

Unconscious symbols can be experienced or only come as a wish or an urge. However, if an individual becomes identified with the symbolic image itself, he or she becomes the victim, condemned to live out the symbol passively rather than to understand it consciously. If it is not conscious, it may be identified with the archetypal psyche and lived out as domineering power and not as positive strength.

Humans need a world of symbols. The relationship of the ego to the symbol is critical. One may identify with the symbol, be alienated from the symbol, or be able to separate from the archetypal psyche, but still remain receptive to the effects of symbolic imagery. The goal of Jungian psychology is to make the symbolic process conscious, or to humanize the archetypes.

This explains some of the differences between Jung's depth psychology and other psychological theories. In Freudian psychology, the id is substitued for transformational archetypal psyche. The id seems to be seen as instinct only, with no consideration for the *images* that lie behind these instincts. It is important to understand the Freudian attitude, since it is shared by most modern schools of psychotherapy. To deny the symbolic inner meaningful life, however, is to deny the possibility of transformation of psychic energy or of humanizing the archetypes in order to lift instinctual energy to a higher level.

The Self* is an a priori inner determinant but can only be experienced at first in relation to the parents. If the ego-Self axis is damaged by parental rejection, the child's ego is weakened and opened to the more negative or evil aspects of life. Often, a parents' rejection of the child is a projection of their own shadow onto the child. This rejection can be experienced by the child as an archetypal rejection by God, or inhuman totality. Thus, deep archetypal guilt occurs and passive victimization becomes part of the fate of the child throughout life.

*When I use the term Self with a capital letter throughout this Jungian study it means center or going beyond self to a new kind of ego consciousness, Higher Self or "God" within, or the center of psychic awareness. When self is in small letters it refers to ego or self but includes both the conscious and the unconscious personalities

At this point, therapy or the complete acceptance of a trusted adult is necessary. Sandplay therapy lets the child or adult directly experience the images of the symbols and thereby transform the images of the self-sacrificing archetype (such as Job) to a more creative image or individual Self. When symptoms of resentment of life's cruelties, such as Job's encounter with God, become deeply embedded, then the individual must recognize the archetype to see the symbolic image behind the symptom and accept the immediate transformation. This experience may still be just as painful, but it now has meaning. Some symbolic life is necessary for psychic healing; otherwise, the ego is alienated and becomes the victim to cosmic anxiety. Understanding the symbols in dreams is another unconscious and conscious way of understanding the victim and the need to experience the opposite sides of life.

Victimization must be understood from an archetypal and collective unconscious point of view, as well as from the objective reality of both instinctual and spiritual factors. The case studies of victims who were able to face, both consciously and unconsciously, the archetypal symbols that appeared in their sandplay therapy clarify how understanding symbols allows victims to witness consciously their pain and suffering and then move on to healing.

Each individual needs to explore, consciously and unconsciously, the possibility that everyone is or has been a victim at one time or another. Many people find it difficult to admit this, especially to recognize that the rage of the victimizer is often unconsciously inside their own self. The abused individual either tries to fight back or withdraws inwardly. In either case, he or she needs outer support, or else his or her victimization will be projected onto the outer world. This is the point at which the inner child (whether adult or child) can become wounded and lose feeling capacity. However, if the victim is strong enough to contain the evil experienced within, the psyche can be healed.

The Inner Child and the Collective Unconscious

Archetypes are all around us in the collective world. Two that require in-depth exploration are the Divine Child and the Great Mother, or mother *imago*. These archetypes relate clearly to child abuse and to the abandonment of the inner child and are receiving a great deal of attention both from modern analysts and psychoanalysts. The abuse of the inner child is only one aspect of victimization, but it is a most important aspect, which until quite recently has been ignored. This study concentrates on ways of humanizing the archetypes, especially of the divine, or inner child.

Perhaps the best human example of the Mother archetype is Mother Teresa of India. She is caring, nourishing, and mothering. Yet, she seems quite sensitive in all her dealings with high officials, politicians, and ordinary people. In addition, she has many friends and followers. Mother Teresa's physical illness seems incidental to her; she simply continues her work—or fate, as she sees it—in a loving way. Clearly, she carries within herself an archetype of divine mother and child. Yet, she is completely human, thus offering a good example of someone who has humanized the archetypes with which she may have been born.

A different negative family archetype is constellated when either or both parents appear to the child as an *all-perfect person*—or, sometimes, as the opposite, the *all evil*, or cruel, mother or father. Other kinds of negative relationships are sometimes sustained by one or the other parent actually seeing himself or herself as the all-perfect or all-evil one.

Some individuals have been known to go through life attached to a *Ghost Lover* archetype—a human being who is not in reality the lover that the other person has projected. An example is that of a woman or man who falls in love with an ideal godlike person. If there is not a complete relationship between them, the lover remains a dream figure and is never actually alive. He or she simply lives in the projection image, or fantasy, of the person who continues to live in love but not in an actual loving human relationship.

Humanizing the Victim Archetype

The road to healing suggests that unless victims humanize and harmonize the inner and outer life (conscious and unconscious) by working with symbols, dream images, active imagination, and ritual, there can be no deep creative living. For healing to take place, both individually and collectively, individuals, including children, must accept some responsibility for their role in the victim-victimizer relationship. Healing occurs when a person who is a victim realizes that these archetypal images of the victim and the victimizer are universal and lie within everyone, for then the connection to the inner child and the self is made possible. At this point, the transformation of the self-sacrificing martyr into hero or warrior is also possible. Archetype, symbol, and myth work together to transform and heal the individual, as this investigation will attempt to show, so that a balance of inner and outer life can be attained.

Jung's concept of the Self helps to explain *humanizing* the archetypes. He states often that the child is born with a Self, the center of each individual. For example, when the child is young and the mother is not available both emotionally and physically, the child will probably form an attachment to an archetypal mother, either the Great Mother, or the evil witch Kali Mother. In this case, humanizing the archetype in therapy would mean becoming able to sort out who the actual mother, father, or companion is and what the victim's own projections are. Removing one's own projectios from another person is a long struggle that involves sacrifice and some pain. In other words, to accept one's own destiny, one must know the self as both *victim* and *victimizer* and to be able to distinguish self (ego) from Self (the Higher Self).

To humanize an archetype, the individual must first have a clear image of how the archetype manifests itself, and in what form. If the individual is in therapy, either analytical or psychoanalytical, he or she may project this negative archetypal image onto the therapist—who hopefully is able to contain (rather than surrender to) the image until the individual can distinguish the objective parent, friend or enemy, and finally relate as a human being. Full healing and transformation cannot take place without conscious submission (not surrender) and acceptance of pain and suffering.

A large part of modern psychoanalytical theory may be attributed to Freud's early work on ego and self. As analysts and psychoanalysts currently reach better understandings of self, much more is being discovered about how to work with the self as the victim or the victimizer, and treatment methods are becoming more effective. Many studies show how victimization within the family is carried on from one generation to the next. Most therapists agree that when a child is victimized and lacks support or understanding from the family, he or she may, in turn, victimize others who are susceptible to being bullied or dominated. Very often a father or mother who has been victimized as a child will victimize his or her own children later in life. Thus, therapists are discovering that it is just as important to treat the victimizer as the victim.

One must understand first that there is a relationship between archetype and victimology, and second that treatment must include the victim's *conscious* sacrifice or pain and submission before the archetypes can be fully humanized. If the circumstances that caused the victimization are too heavy or too collective to bear, or if the individual has not developed a strong enough ego or sense of self, the process of humanizing archetypal images is more difficult. In this case, it is essential to bear the pain alone or with some supportive outer and inner help. Otherwise, the individual must necessarily live a split, or false, life that is unbalanced and unintegrated.

Focus of Later Chapters

Chapter II presents a more detailed discussion of literature relating to victimized children and adults. Some of this literature is correlated to the case studies when it relates to one particular child victim or to a mother who was caught in passive victimization. Chapter III explains the methodology, and Chapter IV tells the story of Job as a Biblical story, as a legend of the human and universal victim, and as a case study. Jung's views on the development of consciousness of man and

God are reviewed in detail, as is the work of Stephen Mitchell (1987), who sees Job as representing suffering for all mankind. This chapter also includes some of William Blakes's images and views of Job as victim. Chapter V gives an account of four child case studies and of one adult case study. Chapter VI summarizes and suggests further possible research in this complicated field.

The case study of John illustrates how a person—in this case, a boy of nine—can be possessed by the archetype of *all-perfect* mother. John was overcome to the extent that he could not accept an ordinary nourishing mother and family until he was finally able to rebuilt a new Self and humanize his own personal archetypes. The case study of Bob illustrates the unconscious archetypal influence projected onto him from birth rejection and abandonment.

Jack's study reveals more of a *God-type* archetype, which so overcame Jack that he took the role of family scapegoat and victim, feeling guilty that he must have done something wrong and thus needed to be punished by family or God.

Suzzi was overwhelmed by two archetypes—the first an *all-perfect* father, who later was transformed into the second archetype, an *all-evil* punishing god who required that she kill herself as sacrifice to this inhuman archetype.

The last case, that of Kate, illustrates archetypes so deep-seated that they were not humanized in the first or second generations; not until the third generation did they become fully transformed. Kate became a passive victim and drifted into a mythological split, trying to live the *all-good mother*. She was able to know only an *all-good God* and and *all-good husband*, and was never able to develop a strong enough ego to heal her own victimization. This study tells how her victimhood affected her life and the lives of her children, grandchildren and great-grandchildren.

Summary and Questions for Further Study

Many research questions still need to be explored. For example, why does the word *victim* seem to be ignored as a subject for research at present, and how did it get lost these past few decades? In the beginning of history, it was related only to religious sacrifices and ritual. Now it seems to be more of a legal term. With the increase of public interest in child abuse, more questions will be asked and, hopefully, answered. We still need to emphasize how to use old and present knowledge more effectively in order to heal both the victim and the victimizer. Perhaps today's most urgent question is how to free the vulnerable lost child within all of us? How can we best treat victims who seem at the mercy of their lives?

Much is known about children theoretically, but little about how to practice these techniques. In addition, parents seem to be undervalued in our present society. However, the archetype of the Child is a symbolic possibility for a new era. Can our society look at today's mechanical, technological age and see its connection to the epidemic of child abuse? Or is society too inflated with power to relate more to the natural forces of life, as our inner and outer lives demand?

To clarify the hypothesis and purpose of this Jungian theoretical study, many questions are raised that will no doubt lead to future research. Some relevant ones for this study are:

a. What are the different forms in which a victim appears as hero, passive, or innocent child?

b. Why are some victims able to overcome their trauma, while others fall into a deep depression?

c. Why do many victims blame themselves and feel deeply guilty for what has happened to them? Why do they feel that they have caused the trauma and are being punished by their parents or by God?

d. Why does the victim often become the victimizer?

e. How does the victim usually experience his or her own victimization?

f. Why do some victims become martyrs while others follow the hero role?

g. What is the history of victimization and how is it related to the collective unconscious and myth?

h. What are some differences between Jungian archetypal therapy and psychoanalytical healing methods of treating the victim?

i. And, most important, how can the individual work more effectively towards humanizing the archetypes, so he or she is not possessed throughout his or her lifetime?

At present there is a need for more collective consciousness of the negative effects of victimization. We must, for example, uncover the motivation behind war and mass violence in our present collective world. On the opposite side, there are the few who work to balance the negative with more positive life forces. It takes only a few people like Mother Teresa, Victor Frankl, and Gandhi to counterbalance some of the greed and evil that is being deposited into the collective unconscious from past generations. At present, others are working quietly behind the scenes, struggling to save endangered species, to ensure the purity of our water, and to deal constructively with other collective problems. Still others are working under very difficult hardships to help communities and individuals in undeveloped countries.

In view of where our Western collective thought has brought humanity, it is no doubt time to recognize the interior Savior Child archetype, in distinction to the more monster-type Inhuman Child archetype that seems to have been let loose in the collective world. Adults need to honor and recognize their own inner wounded and destructive child. This is another way of humanizing the ever-present violent and epidemic forces now so clearly alive and seemingly in command of society today. The achetypes of violent power and destruction are no longer held in check or balance by the opposite forces for good. It may be time for the archetypal Savior Child to be born in a more recognizable form, or for more humans to become acutely conscious of the collective pain and suffering not yet made conscious in our modern world.

II. VICTIM & ARCHETYPE IN THE LITERATURE

Since imagery and metaphor is so vital to understanding archetypal material, this chapter begins with three graphic illustrations of victimization. The three images amplify some of the tremendous complexities involved in comprehending the many archetypes related to victimization.

Kali, Negative Mother
The negative, Dark Mother Kali, is believed to have the power to possess her victims

Cronus Swallowing His Son
This classic rendering depicts Chronus, the father of Zeus, sacrificing one of his sons.

The Sacrifice of Christ's Blood

A very early representation of Christ, showing his blood dripping as
sacrifice for mankind. Blood was a powerful image often emphasized
in religious images of Christ being hung on the cross.

With these powerful collective images in mind, we now review some of literature, including both the classical Jungian and more recent post-Jungian writings, along with a look at Freudian studies in this field. While exploring these studies, this chapter emphasizes the relation of these works to the healing of victims.

Archetypal Symbols in Early Studies

C. G. Jung (1952) and (1953) wrote and later published extensive material about archetypes. In earlier writings he uses the term *primordial image*, but later relates archetype more to the instincts. He holds that at the deeper stratum there are inborn forms of intuition that determine all psychic processes, and thus demand to be taken seriously

According to Jung (1977), instinct and archetype form the collective unconscious, repeating many times that in no way could archetype ever be fully explained or disposed of. Jung further contends that an individual is historical but also a part of the eons of his species. Archetype images can appear in anyone's head at any time and place, he asserts.

Henderson (1967) amplifies this concept. "In order to understand the nature of an archetypal image, it is necessary to experience it subjectively as well as to observe it as an object" (p. 5). Henderson, like many Jungian analysts has learned that there is no need to prove the theory of archetypes; it is everywhere present and simply part of the individual and collective world.

In addition to being everywhere present, archetypal symbols can be accepted or not, according to one's own inner experiences. Marie-Louise von Franz (1973), for example, contends that there is a special archetype that impresses its image so deeply on the personality that the individul is possessed. Henderson also mentions this. In this study, this happens in the case of Kate.

Neither Jung nor Henderson seems to use the term victimization directly. Their comments about archetypes in Jungian phychology, however, help to clarify some of the complications about understanding the influences of archetypes on modern psychology and healing. von Franz (1972) wrote about early creation myths from different cultures. Many of her stories tell how the first human being sacrifices part of his own body to create the world. One well-known myth is of the Chinese god Pan Ku, who sacrifices his eyes to create the Yangtse River and other parts of his body to create the entire land of China.

Many of the early Greek myths tell of a father sacrificing sons to the gods. For example, Zeus offers Ganymede, his favorite young lover, to the mighty eagle. His father, Cronus, swallows one of his sons, see illustration above.

The Old Testament tells of Adam, the first man of the Bible, who sacrifices his rib to create the woman, and thence the human race. The Bible also portrays the story of Abraham, who both loved and feared God to such a degree that he was willing to sacrifice his only son, Isaac. Some individuals see Christ as a victim whose blood is sacrificed for the sins of all mankind.

These myths and the history of the victim throughout the world's civilizations show that victimization has been a part of human life from the very beginning.

Revealing the Victim Archetypes

Two other earlier Jungian analysts, Neumann and Edinger, have written about archetypes as they relate to the victim. Neumann (1962) writes about the development of the feminine when it reaches high enough consciousness to withstand victimization. In the myth of Amor and Psyche, for example, it is only after Psyche becomes more aware, that she changes from the unconscious feminine to the true goddess. Amor changes from the monstrous, inhuman victim lover to the transcendent Eros, or true lover, only after he recognizes his own inner feminine and is healed. It seems that when the Earth Mother, or nourishing mother, is ignored, victimization and violence become stronger. Neither Psyche nor Amor is related to the conscious nourishing mother in the beginning. Both are possessed by archetypal images and remain victims until the archetypes are humanized and each becomes conscious of his or her own fate.

Edinger (1972) writes about ego and archetype and stresses the relationship between ego and Self. "Self is first experienced in projection with the child's parents. It cannot emerge without a parent-child relationship" (p. 39). If ego-Self connection is damaged by deep rejection or shadow projection from the parents, the individual's whole psyche may be damaged permanently. Although Edinger does not use the term *victim*, victimology is clearly implied.

Until quite recently, little pertinent reseach has been done about the victim, at least not under that specific term. However, the word victimization is now being used, especially as a legal category. For example, an article from a meeting of the ROCAP Child Psychiatry Group, held on June 29, 1990, notes the suggestion that *victimization disorder* might be considered for DSM-IV categorization.

Perhaps the rituals of sacrifice in myth and religious rites have been forgotten. However, there has been a revival of many Satanic rituals, which are evolving and being reenacted in the collective world at the present time. These meetings are being reported in newspapers, radio, and television and by therapists who have treated these victims.

Victimization Related to Guilt and Atonement

Cornes (1984), a more recent writer, talks about the possibility of modern therapy using some of the early methods of relieving individuals of guilt. He traces the psychological background of victimization as it applies to melancholia. He begins by mentioning some early myths about cruel mothers, and relates this to object relation studies of the good and bad mother. Babies relate their hunger, when refused the breast, to their own guilt, and this makes them feel like they need to be punished.

Cornes also discusses both Kline and Fordham's definitions of ego-self, especially as related to childhood fantasies of object and image. Both good and bad are present for children from a very early age, he argues. If the opposites are not contained, the individual falls into a state of victimization, wherein depression and the death wish follow.

Cornes' main thesis centers around the Divine or Savior Victim. He traces the history of how religious symbols are used in healing, and how religious rites are used to help the individual feel less guilty. Primitive peoples both feared and loved God, Cornes stated, and early Christians practiced deep lamentations to take away their guilt and fear. Lamentation psalms were used for healing in very early history. Cornes suggests that perhaps some of these old methods might be used to help very depressed individuals today. He traces some of the problems of present-day aloneness, and even sleeplessness and impotence, as arising from the fact that we are cut off from the gods.

A person is just as much out of balance when possessed by the archetype of the Divine One or Chosen One. These individuals have not been able to integrate both the bad and the good Mother. Cornes further states that the child with an undeveloped or weak ego is at the mercy of the shadow. If the shadow is heavier than the more personal evil within the family, the child bears the full weight of the collective or *absolute evil*.

Guggenbuhl-Craig (1990) and many other therapists have noted the recent revival of Satanic cults in many parts of the Western world. These groups carry out gruesome rituals in the worship of Satan. Psychically, Westerners still need atonement rites to help balance the relationships of life, the good and the bad, the conscious and the unconscious. Suffering and pain still seem necessary. Cornes' work shows one side of the victim, the savior or the divine archetype, but his work is incomplete and leaves out a consideration of the evil side, which needs to be balanced with the opposite too good side.

Achieving Balance Between Conscious and Unconscious

Much present clinical work centers around helping patients to balance the relationship between ego and Self, or conscious and unconscious. Suffering without self-pity is essential to both victim and victimizer. The studies of this clinical psychologist and other Jungian research findings clearly suggest that the good and bad in life can be balanced more easily through work with dreams, sandplay, and active imagination. Kalff (1971), working with Sandplay therapy, concluded that there was a balancing and centering of the Self, which is "stabilized in the unconscious of the child at about the age of three and begins to manifest itself in symbols of wholeness" (p. 12).

Other clinical and psychoanalytical techniques and methods seem to work well for more objective or outer personal hardships and traumas. A further step may be necessary as well, and that is to discover and make conscious the inner victim within each individual. Many Jungians explain suicide and deep depression as a negative relationship to the self. If there is a too-harsh mother or father fighting a weak ego, the child will suffer deeply. If a victim with a weak ego encounters an aggressive victimizer, terror and deep pain must be endured and supported in order for soul healing to take place.

Campbell (1988) discusses images and myths and stresses the fact that modern Westerners are out of balance with life, having lost their connection to the gods, rituals, and dreams. He holds that consciousness is raised by myth and meditation, and that each person is the center and the mystery of life. Campbell notes the importance of opposites in life: to be whole one must know both joy and sorrow, light and dark. Campbell explains that healing would be found for both victim and victimizer if more people could accept and live both sides of life.

Even though most of Campbell's work was related to raising the consciousness of Westerners, he was very interested also in parents' everyday attitudes toward children. He often reflected on the fact that parents who were too heavily burdened with pain and guilt themselves often inflicted that suffering onto their own children. He agreed that pain and violence not made conscious would be carried into future generations. He said that mothers need to develop egos strong enough to allow their children to separate consciously and not to live in self-dependence and self-pity.

Universal Victimology and Acceptance of Victimization

The concept of self-pity in relationship to victimization has been studied by many researchers. Some of Victor Frankl's

(1969) concepts about self-pity and universal victimology correlate with Campbell's views. Frankl talks about how necessary it is to not give in to self-pity. He is best remembered for the wonderful spirit he maintained during his many years of incarceration by the Nazis. He was able to recognize the victimhood of all the prisoners but could see the victim archetypes in the guards, as well. He never lost sight of the goodness in life, despite all the hardships he endured from the very harsh fate that seemed to be his journey.

Although the word *victim* is still not found in many psychological indices, a large body of the literature focuses on trauma and other related subjects, such as masochism and the wounded inner child. Psychoanalysts have written several works on the subject recently. Terr (1990), for example, reports the story of the children from Chowchilla who were kidnapped and buried in a bus for many days before being rescued. Terr discovered by following the lives of the victims after the event that despite the experience of shared victimization, each individual viewed the trauma in a distinctly different way. Similarly, Shengold (1989) writes of the serious soul effects of childhood abuse, both to the child and to the families involved. These stories correlate with Miller's (1981) desire to collect truthful information about early victimization of children, and they add a further dimension to this complicated collective problem.

Benjamin's (1988) book on gender domination and victimization explores important questions, also: Why do people submit to authority and derive pleasure from the power that others exert over them? Why is it so difficult for men and women to meet as equals? Why do so many individuals accept the positions of master and slave? Benjamin discusses gender domination as a psychological problem. She suggests that gender identity is deeply ingrained in the child's ego by the age of two. Even at this stage when there is some crossover between the sexes, the father exemplifies the wider outer world. The child must receive the love of both sexes, but, Benjamin believes, mother nurturing is very important, and it is often the mother who holds the child's too powerful aggressiveness when the child is out of control. There must always be room for each individual to have open space, otherwise the child will not be able to discover his or her individual self. It is usually the mother who needs to sustain the tension until healing can happen.

Although Benjamin does not use the words *sacrifice* or *archetype*, these images are deeply embedded in her theory of male and female personality. Male domination goes far back into history and myth, she contends, but both parents must accept their separate roles while at the same time working together and respecting each other fully. If *Powerful Father* and *Weak Mother* archetypes are not constellated too strongly, then the mother can feel her own inner power, and both male and female can be equal in spirit and heart.

Benjamin's book gives an account of feminism at a new level. Her thesis seems to correlate well with those of Neumann (1962), Cowan (1985), and TePaske (1982), all four of whom deal with this subject in great depth, amplifying the Dark Mother archetype. She indicates that if male or female is unable to balance their individual wholeness, then victimization is bound to happen to mother, father, or the entire family. She further states that domination is a two-way process, a system involving both those who submit to power, as well as those who exercise it.

This resonates with the theory explored in this study, which views the healing process of both the victim and the victimizer as everyone's responsibility. The current epidemic of child molestation suggests that too many individuals have lost their inner creative child and are responding from other, more societal events, or perhaps more from unconscious archetypal possession, which is ever-present in the collective world.

Victimology as Ritual or Possession

Some of the newer literature relates to victim in more ritualistic forms. For example, TePaske (1982) discusses rape as ritual. He suggests that while the violence of rape is a problem for men, it is not necessarily the most deviate of men who commit this act. There is, however, a correlation with the socially deprived.

Ever since Eve and Pandora, the responsibility for sexual evil has been projected onto women. TePaske discusses how present-day individuals are having dreams that show violence and rape as deep archetypes in the psyches of both modern men and women. Rapists seem to be possessed by unconscious forces of the Dark Mother or Kali and are overcome by psychotic forces greater than themselves. They project a pure, cruel power onto the other. The real struggle is in finding a union with masculine and feminine within each person's psyche. TePaske implies that women must become more conscious and able to separate from the Great Mother in order to become a separate individual and a human mother. Women need to know their own inner masculine side so they will not be sacrificed unconsciously. If the feminine is caught in unconsciousness, a woman cannot truly know her self-worth. Likewise, the male caught in an archetype of inflated power and violence cannot be whole.

Cowan (1988) amplfies the theme of victim and masochism in similar terms in her study of individuals who are unable to submit consciously to the Higher Self or to a higher power. She cites the Greek myth of Prometheus as an example of a masochistic personality. Prometheus stole fire from the gods to help humankind, and was never able to humble himself to acknowledge the higher power of the gods or his own Higher Self. He suffered inflation and never learned to love his fate. Cowan suggests that although masochism is humbling, it is dedicated to death and thus not healing. A masochist has not learned or experienced what it means to humanize the achetype or to find his or her own journey.

Perera (1986) offers a clear definition of the relationship of scapegoat and victim. She stresses the need for the individual to have a conscious relation to his or her wounds and to feel the pain. Her definition of archetype stresses the motif of collective patterns that emerge in dreams and visions. Healing for the scapegoat means to disengage from the archetype. This can be done by enduring and witnessing the conscious pain, and by being willing to risk change.

This means that fear and rage must be met and suffered: the individual's ego must become active and responsible, even heroic. If the person is in therapy, the analyst must be able to nurture the victimized one, who needs to pass from the enslavement of anger and rage to the transformation of healing. First, however, the hidden self-child must be found and supported. One problem for the scapegoat is not to drift to the opposite side of messiah or savior. Instead, one must witness the suffering as an objective fact of life, both the painful and the joyful. If the demonic accuser is too strong to withstand, the individual may become the passive victim or the overly demanding one and deny his or her own shadow and projections.

Masochism and the Abuse of Children

Currently, mass violence, abandonment, famine, and war are so evident in the collective unconscious that more publicity is being given to the torture and killing of children and adults as world victims. With the rise in prevalence of child abuse, there has been a great deal of interest in the behavior of adult offenders, and of the victims as well. With more awareness of human victimization has come more interest in better treatment methods for both victim and victimzer. However, many questions and misunderstandings remain about both the meaning and treatment of victimization.

Since the word *masochism* is used by both analysts and psychoanalysts in the study of the victim, it is important to note how these two schools of therapy use the term differently. According to Gunderson (1983), the masochistic personality disorder is the repetitious pattern of self-defeating behaviors and relationships that persist despite the patient's complaints of being victimized. Self-defeating people have a sense of weakness about situations that bring them misery. Masochism has now been included in DSM-III-R for clinical use.

Guggenbuhl-Craig (1990), in discussing some records recently found, told the audience about child persecutions in early-day rites. These records showed how children were tortured in all kinds of horrible ways. These tortures were not only of children, but often self-inflicted by many religious men and women as well. Relating these to present-day masochism, he further stated that the instigators of these rites were mostly very wealthy, influential, and religious men.

Guggenbuhl-Craig emphasized the present need to deal with collective unconscious archetypes. Although he found in his recent travels many excellent people attempting to help abused children, he is deeply concerned about the need to uncover the story behind so much mass victimization. Through his explorations, he determined that the key factor in abuse is rage. He went so far as to say that the psyche itself is the main cause of abuse; in other words, that the capacity to abuse is within all of us. Most people prefer to believe that only bad people do bad things and that only good people do good things.

At this point in his lecture, Guggenbuhl-Craig shifted his focus to discuss the fact that the world is changing from a patriarchal to a matriarchal society. Much hate and rage towards fathers, both human and archetypal, still remains. We have all been abused by God or tyrannical fathers, he explained, and part of evil comes from nature itself. The Heavenly Father is often projected onto the human father, just as the Divine or all-perfect Child is sometimes mistaken for the not-so-innocent human child.

On a more hopeful note, Guggenbuhl-Craig stated that perhaps the symbol of the Divine or Savior Child will bring in a new era, and that this symbol will provide a balance to the collective rage. His theory is that it is necessary to hold and contain the rage, which is deeper and stronger than any one individual, at least until better methods of healing are found. This statement correlates well with the present study.

According to Guggenbuhl-Craig's thesis, it is important for each individual to keep in touch with his or her vulnerable child. Victimization is thus the responsibility of all individuals, including children, to some degree. If collective responsibility is shared, then the individual victim feels less guilt and can direct more inner power toward facing his or her own pain and suffering.

Reclaiming the Inner Child

Guggenbuhl-Craig seems to preface Abrams' (1990) view that a person must first learn to know, experience, and reclaim his or her own inner child in order to understand child or adult victimization. The inner child concept offers Jungians and Freudians one bridge to better understand how the victim often turns victimizer, and how victimization is a problem for everyone. As a unifying symbol for the Self and wholeness, the inner child can become the link to healing, not only for the abused child, but for the needed integration of inner and outer child in adults as well.

To amplify his theme, Abrams (1990) invited 37 well-known therapists, analysts, and pschoanalysts to write more fully on the subject. This study focuses on excerpts from two post-Jungians, R. E. Rothenberger and R. Stein, and four post-Freudians, E. Erickson, T. Reik, S. Osherson, and A. Miller. Erickson (1990), for example, stated that Freud saw that the real value of psychoanalysis was to improve parenting. In teaching us to recognize the *demonic evil* in children, he urged us not to smother the creative good. In this way, Freud is a pioneer in self-healing: "Generations to come may well need to appreciate and to preserve more genuine childlikeness in order to avoid utter cosmic childishness" (p. 287).

Reik (1990) adds that the child is the father of the man: "In realiy, there are three persons in the consultation room of the psychoanalyst: the analyst, the patient as he or she is now, and the child who continues to exist within the patient" (p. 289)

Osherson (1990) speaks of child and parent in a similar vein. The psychoanalyst must search for the child in the man, in himself, and in others. He suggests that male vulnerability in relationships can be traced back to early childhood experiences of separaton and loss. Osherson states that "men have a task, to heal the wounded parent within, in order to become more nurturing parents to their inner and outer children" (p. 295).

From a Jungian point of view, Abrams (1990) writes about the eternal child that we all carry within ourselves. He states, "As a symbolic and poetic reality, the inner child appears in our imaginations, our dreams, our art, and in mythologies throughout the world. This image represents renewal, divinity, a zest for life, a sense of wonder, spontaneity, and immortality. As such, the inner child is a uniting symbol and brings together the separated or dissociated parts of the individual personality" (p. 1). Abrams goes on to say that the inner child is the soul of the person and the primordial image of the Self, the very center of our individual being.

Abrams' selections center around six major themes: (1) mythic images of the inner child; (2) abandonment; (3) the narcissistic disturbance; (4) the wounded child; (5) realizing the child's gifts and vitality; and (6) revitalization of child-rearing practices. These major themes also appear in the articles reviewed below.

Rothenberg (1990) writes about abandonment, or the orphan archetype. The orphan image appeals to the young person who undertakes his rite of passage, leaving the security and protection of the family. The adolescent who loses a parent is doubly affected. Sometimes the orphan begins to act like the witch or bully and becomes the oppressor. This suggests that the orphan is possessed by the negative side of the parent-child archetype. "If the orphan finds a surrogate mother in life or therapy, two opposing opposites may be constellated, one a step-mother witch and the other the positive-mother spirit" (Rothenberg, p. 95). One is potentially destructive and the other potentially healing. The individual must feel hurt, anger, pain, and sadness before assuming more responsibility for himself. In this regard, Rothenberg's position corresponds to the case study of John in Chapter V of this discussion.

Post-Freudian Alice Miller (1981) focuses on the outer child, but is also very interested in the wounded child within—the one who suffers through cruel abuse by parental and authority figures. She believes that the truth about our childhood is stored up in our body; we can repress it but not alter it. In other words, child abuse has lifelong effects.

Miller's work with children who have been molested and wounded can and does have positive results. However, this therapist's clinical work with children has found that many victims and victimizers simply do not fit the categories Miller uses for healing.

What are the causes that seem to push some individuals who have been deeply traumatized into such deep depression that there appears to be no return? Is it as Stein (1990) conjectures; that the cause of victimization lies in the victimizer's loss of contact with his or her inner creative child, and ability to respond only from the badly wounded and angry inner child? Based on this therapist's clinical practice with children and adults, sandplay has been a means to reconnect victims to their inner child, enabling them to confront and accept inner images that were previously unconscious.

Stein's (1990) views about the wounded child and child abuse are very different from Miller's. Stein states that child abuse always reflects a lack of connection to the internal or psychic child. Abuse is perpetuated internally by a loveless, critical superego that has no understanding or respect for the inner child. "When an adult suffers from a deep spirit/flesh, mind/body, love/sex split, he or she will often fall under the compulsive power of the sexual drive to literalize those images" (p. 193). "Healing does not lie in attempting to overcome these perverse desires, but in being able to experience fully the incestuous desires in imagery. In this way, the sexual drive is gradually transformed, and the child (inner and outer) can be loved, honored, and respected as a unique being" (p. 196).

Recent Dissertation Abstracts on Victim and Archetype

A wider range of information on victim and archetype comes from 22 dissertation abstracts written between the years 1980-1990. Of these, seven were chosen as most pertinent to the topic of humanizing archetypes. Pagnucci (1981), for example, in reviewing Deledda's novels, states that they are based on a Biblical pattern of sin, suffering, expiation, and redemption. This theme resembles that of Cornes (1985). To Pagnucci, all of Deledda's characters are subject to evil by the very nature of their existence. The protagonist moves from error to repentance and finally to symbolic redemption, ordered by the archetypal motif of the journey of the psyche.

Elefant-Dietz (1981) used the Minotaur as a symbol for archetype. She explains that it can be projected onto different representations and has been conceived of as sacrificial victim as it changes forms. This relates to the time when young virgins were sacrificed to the bulls in early Cretan mythologies.

Two other important themes emerge in these dissertations on archetype and victim. They address the splitting of the feminine psyche and *bound children*. According to Hampsey (1982), all of William Blake's poetry shows that the parents' tyranny over the children is actual as well as symbolic. Blake (1982) repeatedly stressed the binding action of experience over innocence. The archetypal man (Rebellious Son) is trapped and tyranized by a godlike father, priest, or king.

Two dissertations about victimization written by women, Martha Harrell (1987) and Carolyn Dickinson (1989), are also significant. Harrell states that although women of the 1980s are professionally competitive and assured, in intimate relations with men they are sadly and painfully masochistic and appear as puppets. This split can be traced to primal relationships with parents. When the mother knows herself as weak and a victim of a patriarchal culture, she is apt to marry a man on whom she can be dependent, leaving no safe place for the child. Often there is the trauma of alcohol or death in the family to cope with, as well. So the child splits in order to sustain the mother; the child is thus forced to live a false self while her true self hides. Harrell used Sandplay therapy and fairy tales to help the patient constellate the hidden self back into life.

Dickinson used three of George Elliot's stories to challenge the cultural myths supporting the status quo of women. To dispose of old myths, she states, we must displace them by new ones, associating heroines with archetypal figures of heroic proportions. Next, she emphasizes that we must now show women characters who are moving from victimized degradation to creative autonomy.

Peroomian (1989) compares Armenian literary responses to catastrophe with the Jewish experience. He discusses four American writers, both Jewish and Armenian, who write about genocide. Peroomian attempts to create some truth of the imagery of the Armenian view compared to the Jewish holocaust. Most Jewish writers, he found, illuminated human suffering, atrocity, and a will to endure and survive under inhuman circumstances. He compares the persistence of painful memories among both Jewish and Armenian survivors and finds that both groups are able to turn their victimization experiences into creative artistic works. While this account demonstrates the uniqueness of each of their experiences in terms of circumstances, it also shows how both cultures transformed tragedy into art.

An earlier abstract by Perlman (1986) related very closely to Peroomian's. Perlman states that in order to allow Hiroshima a proper place in memory, we must allow for weakness, suffering, and defeat. In contrast to this, modern cultures have valued only strength, health, and victory. Hiroshima signifies the remembrance of the place of death in the psyche versus immortality. Perlman further states that because of our technological power, our present culture must in some way painfully suffer the memory of *nuclear death* if an actual future nuclear holocaust is to be avoided. This hypothesis closely relates to the thesis that pain, suffering and submission, are necessary for true, or soul healing.

Some Differences in Post-Jungian and Post-Freudian Theories

One of the better known post-Jungians is Andrew Samuels. Some of his studies relate to this subject, especially in terms of his interest in building bridges between post-Jungian and post-Freudian theorists. Samuels (1985) suggests that the study of self is of prime importance in most theories and that it surely relates to victim. Self is an inner voice that tells each individual how to live in order to balance conscious and unconscious. Victims, unable to humanize the archetypal images, are forced to connect directly to the archetype itself. For example, if a child becomes possessed by an over balance of either the Good Mother or the Bad Mother, he or she cannot face the actual realities of life and becomes the victim. In Jungian analysis, the victim needs to become conscious of his problems, develop a strong transference, suffer and feel the pain inwardly, and then acknowledge and experience the transformation of the opposites to a more balanced life. Samuels suggests that the archetypal pattern is inherited, even though the content can vary. There are times, for example, when an event and the archetype can become harmonious as though each knew what the other was doing from the beginning. There is always a built-in polarity between positive and negative aspects of emotions as well as experience; in other words, almost everything in life has two aspects. Samuels and many Jungians use the snake image as example of both instinctive and transformational, or as an archetypal opposite. Many analysts also agree that Self pursues unity, order, and totality. Samuels' real contribution is his clear way of charting the primary differences or oppositions between the theories of major schools of psychology. He also includes differences between classic and post-Jungian theories.

In this therapist's experience, when an individual's personal experiences do not bring about the human aspects of the archetypes, he or she is forced to connect directly to the archetype itself. Instead of living fully, the person then lives in archetypal imagery and plays a role that is not quite real or whole. This concept of self and self-awareness seems very much tied in with Samuels' theory of Self and archetypal self. In the Sandplay case studies described in Chapter V, most of the children do suffer their fate and are healed. The mother who is possessed by victimization, as von Franz (1973) suggests, also suffers deeply. However, she never has the family support to strengthen her own weak ego, so she continues to live an archetypal and unconscious, or passive life, for many years.

Ego and Self

The main differences in how Jungians and Freudians understand and treat victims is due more to disagreements about language than anything else. Therapists from both fields are showing more interest in the inner child. However, an obvious difference between the two is the way in which they interpret self. Freudians view self more as an objective or personal self, while Jungians see it as the center, unity, or totality of personality.

Samuels (1985), a post-Jungian, states that the self can be seen as the ordering of feelings about one's self. This image is developed in infancy and dos not require ego-comprehension to take effect. In Jungian analysis, the victim may have lost his centered sense of self so he needs to develop a strong transference, suffer and feel the pain inwardly, and then acknowledge and know the opposites in order to live a more balanced life.

Stern (1985) says that the self is the heart of philosophical speculation on human nature. Sense of self and its counterpart, the sense of other, are universal phenomena that profoundly influence all our social experiences. Development of senses of the self is going on all the time. However the sense of self comes into existence at certain formative phases: *birth to two months, emergent self; two to six months for sense of core self; seven to fifteen months for inter-subjective self; and eighteen to thirty months for the verbal sense of self* (p. 273). Stern believes that there is a definite stage in which different senses of self do appear, whereas Jung insists that Self is present at birth.

Post-Freudian Winnicott (1964), a well-known object-relations expert, and Edinger (1972), a follower of Jung, express somewhat similar ideas about self. Winnicott states that there is no trauma outside the omnipotence of individuals—everything is under the ego's control. He is more interested in infancy and sees infant care and maternal care—*the good mother*—as one. The infant ego is strong only if it is supported by mother care. Poor infant care leads to problems for the adult later on. The infant must give the first signal for separation.

Edinger (1972) sees a spiralling connection between ego and self throughout life. The first half of life is concerned with ego-self separation and the second half with ego-self reunion. He feels that we are born in a state of inflation (ego identification with the self). *No ego consciousness exists; it is all in the unconscious. Self is born, while ego is made* (p. 7). Edinger's theory seems to relate to Winnicott's *all good mother*, who lives in a kind of symbiosis with the infant. The mother, as well as the child, must be ready to separate and help the child to separate—a view that is shared by both post-Jungians and post-Freudians. If separation does not occur positively, alienation and even psychoses can occur. In short, the individual may become victim.

Neumann (1962) identifies clear stages of child development. He speaks of the early, uroboric phase of child development as a period of minimum discomfort and tension and of maximum well being, security, and unity of Self and world. The first experience of the self for both the boy or girl is bound up with the mother (p. 203). This seems comparable to Winnicott's and Ogden's (1986) early stages of infancy development. Neumann states further that the child's earliest relationship with his or her mother is unique, since it occurs before the tension of the I-thou development of personality. This sets its imprint on all future development and is a source of lasting nostalgia, which can leave both progressive and regressive effects on the adult. Ogden similarly explains that when the child is able to deposit the more negative aggressive aspect of him or herself onto the mother, this is not only a defensive projection; it also contains the beginnings of a developmental process. The mother must be able to contain a part of this negativity in order for the child to develop a more balanced self.

Meyrink's (1975) work is also relevant to this study regarding Jungian individuation theory. While this story is about the life of one man, *Golem*, it is actually based on a Jewish archetypal and autonomous figure who causes the narrator to have evil things happen to him. This folk figure was originally made from clay or mud and would come to life when the word GOD was spoken. However, he was without soul and could not speak. In other words, he too was a victim. Some authorities related the Golem to the first Adam, who was originally a giant, according to many authorities (von Franz,1972 p. 99).

Russack (1977) relates the story of the individual author Meyrink, to the path of individuation in Jungian analysis. The narrator goes through many hardships, reviews his life in a conscious way, and is finally able to reconcile the opposites in his life and thus connect his ego to self and Self in a balanced way. He meets death and life, but chooses life and is finally transformed. Meyrink's life story certainly parallels the stories of modern-day victims in their struggle to acknowledge consciously that they are suffering from victimization. Before they can transform their pain they must first make it conscious and suffer it objectively; only then can life be transformed for them into a more creative existence. At the same time, as Russack implies, it is important to acknowledge the victimizer and to be able to contain parts of the negative evil until some healing and consciousness has taken place for both the victim and the victimizer.

III. CASE STUDY AS METHODOLOGY

The methodology utilized in this study draws on Jungian theory. It is qualitative, theoretical, and descriptive. The writer is affected by Jungian analysis, and many years of training in both analytical and psychoanalytical theory. Case study method is validated by many esteemed analysts and psychoanalysts. Although Jungians do not usually collect large bodies of statistics as proving grounds for a theory, they constantly research newer methods of working with individuals and better ways of understanding the unconscious and the conscious. Jung, as far back as 1916, wrote a complete book on one case study alone. It has been republished several times, the latest, Jung (1956).

Jung's Case Study of Miss Miller

In this extensive case study of *Miss Miller*, Jung uses dream and vision analysis, along with active imagination, to explain the need for studying psychic reality as well as everyday events. He begins by explaining that dreams in early analysis bring out critical evaluations of the patient's conscious impression of the doctor and often contain erotic comments that regress back to the father image. By recreating the child image, Miss Miller was able to evade the repressed conflict in her consciousness but not in her dreams and visions. She called her first vision, after a sleepless night, the hymn of creation, and Jung related it to an old myth of the moth and the sun god. Jung stated that Freud would have related this libido to sexuality. Jung, however, saw this as sexual and also as mythological representations for light and sun, thus giving a possibility of life force energy. He further states that this libido energy starts as far back as the infant with his or her sucking in rhythm.

Miller's third vision was of a Peruvian Indian, which Jung calls the hero or demon. This archetype is amplified in many myths and is now a part of the collective unconscious. Freud related symbol formations as preventors to the primary incest tendency. Jung owns the fact that myths can arise as barriers against incest, but also can explain rebirth and transformation. He adds that the effects of incest taboos do stimulate the creative imagination. Symbols are grounded in the unconscious archetype and are numinous and autonomous.

Miller's next visions are of trees, ships, and other images of life and death. Her last visions ended in chaos, illustrated by an infant calling *wa-na* or *ma-ma*. Miss Miller was unable to detach from her childhood father and mother consciously. She was not able to integrate the whole libido, which is needed for the battle of life. Her deep-seated problems were collective and not under the control of a conscious mind. She was unable to think symbolically, and to integrate the dissociative tendencies of the unconscious into the conscious. This study follows the methodology as explained in the case of Miss Miller, using archetypal images, symbols, myth, and active imagination as treatment in sandplay therapy. This method helps objectify the unconscious symbols as they appear spontaneously in the psyche and in the sandtray.

Case Study as Method in Other Disciplines

Different writers have used case study as methodology. Edelson (1988) states that clinical practice is seen as stimulating because it is the source of otherwise inaccessible phenomena. He adds that he doubts that statistical analyses are applied in a neutral manner. Edelson also asserts that *the case study can be an argument about the relation between hypothesis and evidence* (p. 266).

Yin (1989) relates that case study method is used to explain the links in real life interventions and to describe the real life context with no clear single set of outcomes known. Yin further states that case study is an empirical inquiry that investigates contemporary phenomena within real life context. Case studies explore the problems or issues raised; they ask good questions but do not attempt to give complete answers. Since the aim of qualitative research is to understand fully the structure and meanings of experience, a limitation needs to be placed on the number of variables to be analyzed.

Guntrip (1975) emphasizes that theory is rooted in our psychopathology. He states *that theory of the functioning of the personality should be a self-evident impossibility* (p. 67).

In comparing quantitative and qualitative research, Isaac and Michaels (1977, p. 14) state that experiential (subjective) research is commonly seen as more robust. Possible cause-effect relationships were investigated with one or more experimental groups to one or more control groups not receiving the treatment.

Fordham (1985) uses a case study to describe an infant interacting with its mother. He concludes that *if you look only for causes, the facts fly out the window* (p. 6).

According to Hancock (1989), qualitative research approaches are particularly well-suited to areas of inquiry in which little is known. Instead of beginning to study such areas with abstract categories, qualitative approaches begin with questions grounded in the concrete experience of the researcher as well as what might apply from related literature.

This study on the archetype of victim amplifies some of other researchers' work and evolves from many years of studying and working directly with children and adults, many of whom have been victimized. The key aim is to find a deeper archetypal understanding of the subject of victim. Though victimization has been a part of the human culture from the beginning of time, as research shows, little is known about how and why an individual becomes a *possessed* victim or why victimization is repeated in families inter-generationally.

The methodology employed in this study is the use of direct case study following the Jungian theory of using archetypal images, active imagination, and metaphors, to help objectify the unconscious symbols as they appear spontaneously in the psyche and in sandplay therapy.

This study uses four case studies with children from the author's own clinical and experiential material, and from her past 20 years of clinical practice as a Jungian therapist. This work also uses the case of one adult who was overwhelmed by the evil power of the collective unconscious. This victim was unable to find complete healing and wholeness so that the second and third generations following her had to carry, hold, and finally make conscious the archetypes not made conscious in her own lifetime. The four children and the daughter of the possessed adult victim are treated in the experiential process method of sandplay therapy.

In addition to the above case studies, the story of Job is presented as a case study. Job is the universal victim who is ultimately able to contain the pain and grief of many individuals. In the beginning, Job is able to see God but unable to hear him. He takes the role of all victims possessed by evil power.

The method of using sandplay case studies is relevant and open to comparison with other analytical or psychoanalytical theory and practice. It is used in this study to help more individuals rethink some of the present concepts about healing methods for the victim. Although archetypes cannot be proven or disproven at this point in time, it is enough to experience this phenomenon and to understand what happens in the unconscious and conscious of the patient's psyche.

To understand the whole picture of healing, one needs to see and understand relationships. It is inadequate to rationalize, categorize, or pigeonhole evidence only. This therapist is more interested in describing and understanding how the patient feels about his or her victimization; in other words, in studying people as subjects of their own experiences. This is an empirical study of actual lives, in terms of qualitative analysis; not reduction or interpretation.

The meaning of experiences is researched, but not to make a study of facts and figures. The work is not presented as coming from expert authority, but rather as a *sharing and learning* kind of work, between the researcher and subject, backed up by theory.

The most important need at present is to find a common language between modern Jungians and Freudians. The content of this investigation includes a search for a clearer theory of victim and better methods of understanding and relating to the individual as he or she experiences victimization.

Theory and practice need to go together in any therapy. Using a qualitative Jungian theoretical methodology is the objective of this research. Demonstrating phenomena about archetype and victimization is difficult indeed, and it is especially hard to separate out personal biases. Archetypal images have long been studied, but not directly in relation to the deep soul healing of victimization

Freud uses dream analysis in his clinical practice but stresses immediate interpretation. He searches ways of making the unconscious conscious, but his approach is different from that of Jung. Freud's main emphasis seems to be predominantly that of finding better ways of overcoming resistance. Jung, on the other hand, is more interested in finding out what causes resistance. Dreams can be understood by accepting and being open to the images that they produce. Both Freud and Jung are aware of the importance of objective reality.

Schwartz-Salant (1989) states that psychoanalytic literature describes patients in terms of psychotic and neurotic mechanisms. This is very useful as it alerts us to pay attention to helpless parts of the patient. If we underevaluate this, or think of it only as something to change, we are not opening the path to potential healing. Jungians go further into the depth of the chaos to find the structure and the energies of the archetypes.

self and Self

Both analysts and psychoanalysts seem to agree that one of the main differences between them relates to the meaning of self and Self. Quoting from Schwartz-Salant (1989, p. 91), H. Guntrip (1969) suggests that a *piece of the original oneness splits from its fusion with the libidinal-ego, to form a fourth part, the so-called "regressed ego" or the "true self"*. Schwartz–Salant feels that most of the object relation followers, including Guntrip, leave out what Jung conceives of as the autonomy of the archetypes as the psyche's ordering structures; they regulate fantasy and structure dream life. Sharp (1991) defines Self as the archetype of wholeness and the regulating center of the psyche; a transpersonal power that transcends the ego (p. 119).

The rich body of data generated by this formative research suggests that qualitative approaches are fruitful in pursuing deeper meanings of complicated phenomena. By using case studies as amplification, some of this material on victimization can be validated and better understood at the experiential level of consciousness. Interpreting sandplay pictures is clarified in the individual case studies that follow. The images of each child's sand pictures and the symbols presented are summarized. It is important, however, to realize that only the individual experiencing the pain and joy of producing the sand picture can give a true account of what it means to heal his or her psyche.

The case studies chosen for this study have the advantage of giving a clearer perspective of their human lives 15 years after their original therapy. This relates to Edelson (1988), that one's history is relevant and tied to psychoanalytic theory. If we as clinicians immerse ourselves in understanding our own psyches, as well as applying our knowledge to patients, a better theory of the structure and functioning of all individuals evolves.

The research questions raised and identified in Chapter I (p. 10) are amplified more in Chapters IV and V. Questions about why individuals feel so guilty as victim—why victim often becomes victimizer—and how archetypes can be humanized are all fully explored in the case studies of the children and of the one adult, as well as in the story of Job. For example, following the developmental stages of the children described in this study, a process in which the images of archetypes of victim are finally humanized, shows that lasting healing does take place. Bob (Case Study #4) shows how a child at the early age of six, having experienced rejection and abandonment at a very early age, starts to act out his own victimization on the other children. With conscious, adoptive parents and sandplay therapy, he strengthens and transforms his psyche to become a more human and loving individual instead of becoming a victimizer.

Job as Case Study

Job's story (Chapter IV) can be seen as a case study if looked at in a more inner, symbolic way. Some writers have said that victimization such as Job's can also be understood personally as severe illness involving emotional disturbance. All the characters in the story portray some aspect of Job as individual man—for example, the friends, who become the accusers, represent the judgmental side of Job. Satan and God then represent the opposites that he is struggling with. The family represents unconsciousness in the beginning and consciousness at the end.

Job takes on the pain and suffering of all mankind and, by submission to a higher power, is healed. He never becomes the victimizer nor does he feel guilty.

Kahn (1975) states that Job finds his own cure to his illness. Individual psychopathology comes, he states, from cultural maladjustment and critical situations that have come into being today.

The story of Job relates to the unconscious erupting of archetypes on to the individual. Surely, a conscious God would not have been so unjust to an upright man. Still, that is the story. The simple story or myth of Job has lasted through these many generations, and its theme is centered on the archetype of victim.

Summary

Final answers to the research questions that arise in this study are impossible and it is not the purpose of this research to answer them. Some conclusions can be stated, however. First, there are many kinds of victim and depths of meaning for each. Deeper definitions and understandings still need to be explored and other methods of healing must be developed (see further definitions in the glossary). Second, the effects of the collective unconscious have often been ignored in psychotherapy, and this is a rich field for study and deep understanding. Finally, theory, facts, and figures are important when balanced in study for objective reality. The most pertinent need is for better communication between the different schools of psychology, both in meaning and methodology. It is hoped that this researcher's hypothesis, of victim and archetype, is verified. There may still be a need for more concise statements about how healing actually takes place in Jungian therapy and in this study of sandplay specifically.

IV. JOB AS A LITERARY WORLD ARCHETYPAL VICTIM

The story of Job is an example of both universal suffering and personal victimization. It substantiates one of the core ideas of this study, that victimization has existed in the world from the beginning of time. One question that facilitates a modern understanding of victimization is this: Why is so much mass violence erupting in individuals and groups in connection with present victimization? Is this a result of archetypes erupting from the past collective unconscious? How can deep healing occur for the individual overwhelmed by victimization?

When an archetype is not made conscious, or humanized, it drops back into the world psyche of collective unconsciousness. To help clarify this concept more fully, it is necessary to trace some of the early myths and literature about victim and how it became an important part of our history and culture.

Therefore, this early chapter explores the Bible story of Job to show how the archetype of victim has been carried through the many levels of conscious development of mankind and God consciousness as well. When Job was able to see God's face and the split in his nature, there had to be a change in the person of old Yahweh. Job never doubted the totality of God—a totality of inner opposites. He knew that God loved humans, but he never understood His injustice and lack of loving kindness towards Job, as an individual.

The Story of Job

The story of Job is a Jewish archetypal legend, according to Mitchell (1987), and it carries the suffering of all mankind as well as that of the individual. The basic story of Job, as summarized here is taken from the Book of Job (1952, pp.525-562). The story is divided into two parts.

Part I (p. 525)

> There was a man in the land of Uz whose name was Job and that man was blameless and upright, one who feared God and turned away from evil. There was born to him seven sons and three daughters. He had seven thousand sheep, three thousand camels, five hundred yoke of oxen, five hundred she-asses and very many servants; so this man was greatest of all the people of the East. Each year the sons held a banquet and invited the sisters to the feast. When the festivities were over Job would purify each of them for fear they had sinned and cursed God in their hearts.

Part II (p. 526)

> One day the sons of God came before the Lord and Satan came also. The Lord asked Satan where he had come from and he said, "from going to and fro on earth." The Lord asked him if he had observed Job, a man of perfect integrity who feared God. Satan said he had, but reminded God that first he had blessed Job and his possessions. "If you take them away and touch all he has, he will curse you." The Lord then told Satan that all was in his hands, but that he was not to kill Job. Satan left.

From that day on, Job became a victim in every sense. All of his family were killed, except his wife. All his possessions were destroyed. Still Job responded: "Naked I came from the womb and naked I'll return—May the Lord be blessed." Next, Satan demanded that Job's own flesh be tortured in every possible way. This was done but still Job praised God.

Next, Job's friends came and sat with him for a while, but they blamed him for his misfortunes, insisting he had done

some wrong against God and was being punished. Finally, Job
cursed himself and wanted to die, as he could not live with the
horrible physical and emotional anguish. However, he still
insisted on his own innocence, and finally demanded that God
listen to him. He became every man's grief and insisted on an
audience with God, whom he still truly loved.

At last God appeared out of the whirlwind and spoke to Job:
"Where were you when I created the world? Can you show the
Hawk how to fly? Will you tackle the Beast that I made? Hope
is a lie" (Job verses 38, 39, 46, 47). Job responded that he had
heard of God with his ears but now he could see with his eyes,
saying, "Now I will be quiet" (Job verse 42). God cursed Job's
friends but Job begged for their forgiveness, so God forgave
them. He restored all of Job's possessions and his family. He
gave each of the daughters names, thus bringing functional
healing into the archetypal feminine heart. The feminine has
always been related to healing, since it relates to the Earth, or
Nourishing, Mother.

The ending of the legend is so different from the beginning
that many authorities have said that these two parts of the story
were written by different authors. Jung (1952) explains this
dilemma by relating the steps of the all-unconscious Yahweh,
the God that Job was able to see but not hear, to a development
of consciousness on the part of the individual and of God. He
states further that later Jesus, God's son, chose to become man
and was sacrificed. Jesus was too perfect, not whole, having
been born by immaculate conception. So the great need for a
nourishing female as a companion counterpart of the Lord was
still overlooked.

At the present time it seems that man and woman still need
to become more conscious of their own evil and to know the
two sides of God's nature. Humans must recognize also the
deep need of a mediator before any real integration can occur,
allowing God and humankind to become conscious of each
other and more closely related. To this therapist, Self is this
connection of humans to God, or the *other*. Yahweh forgot his
own omnipotence, and this may explain the separation of God
from his feminine partner in Heaven. These statements are

related also to submission to a Higher Self, in order for the victim to be healed. It may be true that the bride of Christ, or the feminine, must become an equal partner to God. Then, real consciousness and healing could occur, closing the split between body and soul, as Campbell (1988) talks about in great depth.

Meier (1981) expresses this same idea by saying that psychic truth can not be proved or disproved. A good image of understanding of this phenomenon is to allow the possibility of undeserved suffering to happen. An example is when a person is able to witness the birth of a crippled child and still believe in God and the goodness of life.

Campbell tells us that Westerners have lost their gods within. As a result they cannot participate deeply in both sorrow and joy. Modern men and women, in following the pattern of Christianity, he contends, started out with a split, with sin as motive, God against man, which is also the story of Job. So Christianity has left out the opposites of both dark and light as necessary for life. Campbell mentions repeatedly that Jesus actually danced to his own death. In other words, he not only understood his own fate as victim but also knew both the opposites of joy and sorrow and the need to accept them.

Campbell sees pain and suffering as necessary elements of life for a more balanced consciousness; however, he does not condone all martyrdom or self-pity. Job's willingness to submit transformed his life from victim to wholeness. He criticized the injustice of God's actions, but he also accepted his own fate in the end; thus a change could occur and his family and possessions be restored. Other writers, for example Nagel (1954), also state that Sophia, or feminine instinct, was left out. However, according to Blake, the feminine spirit is added, when Job's three daughters are given names and inheritances equal to the sons. This brings consciousness one step further towards complete life but not perfect existence. Understanding the story of Job foreshadows a clearer picture and deeper knowledge of victim today. The story may explain more clearly how the more violent archetypes of mass violence and rape are erupting into present consciousness from the past collective unconsciousness.

Stephen Mitchell's Account of Job

Mitchell (1987) relates the Bible story of Job to a parable of the post-Holocaust age and says that Job becomes every man's grief for all human misery, not just for his own pain. Mitchell maintains that a question is answered that even Job would not have dared to ask: "God does not hear Job, but Job sees God?" (p. XVIII). He faced evil and saw the vast wonder of love. Suffering and joy are both a part of life. The victim needs to experience both these aspects of life for healing. Job truly loved God but was outraged at His injustice to himself.

Mitchell calls the Book of Job a paradox in that it is the greatest Jewish work of art, yet its hero is a gentile. He goes on to say that there is no evidence about who the author was, where he came from, or when he wrote. The theme of this legend is the great Jewish one: the archetypal theme of victim. This, according to Mitchell, is what makes Job the central parable of our post-Holocaust age and gives great urgency to its deep spiritual power.

TePaske (1982) writes on the same theme of unconscious victim, referring mostly to violence and rape as victimization. He feels that rape is a problem for men even though sexual evil has been projected onto women. It must now be studied as an intra-psychic event in order to know the archetypal root of sexuality. Rapists seem possessed by the dark collective forces of the Dark Mother.

The real struggle is in finding a union with masculine and feminine within each man and woman's psyche. It seems that the Nourishing Earth Mother has been lost to modern mankind. If so, then the victim and victimizer exist without feeling and are becoming even more powerful and violent.

TePaske uses Kali as an example of the archetypal Dark Mother. Sometimes individuals may be overcome by psychotic forces greater than themselves. They may project a pure, cruel power onto others. He gives the example of Eldridge Cleaver, who, originally a pacifist and a gentle person, became possessed unconsciously by dark forces and began to rape many women, black and white. Later he had a vision of Christ's face in the moon, changed completely, and became a very religious person. TePaske states that since rape may carry with it a desire to sacrifice, and to find the lost wounded child, it could possibly become a transforming function but only if the negative side is made conscious and transformed. True suffering and sacrifice and forgiveness would need to be part of the process. Each man and woman must find his or her individual way to know true Self.

Neumann (1967) points out the same theory as seen through myth. Psyche became more conscious by enduring many trials and suffering. She changed finally from the unconscious feminine to a very conscious immortal goddess. Amor changed from the monstrous lover to the transcendent god Eros, himself. Neumann feels that the anima, or feminine element is the transforming element for most healing.

If the gods, especially Eros, have indeed disappeared, then both man and woman must seek their own true psyches and move toward a consciousness of an inner Self for healing. This may be possible through therapy only or self-actualization at a deeper inner level. Dreams and other mythological connections suggested by Campbell and Neumann can show the way.

William Blake's Images

Raine (1970, 1971) states that William Blake rejects the traditional interpretation of the Book of Job as a pact between God and Satan to test Job. Instead, Blake sees all the actors as parts of Job himself. The devil is the accuser within, and Job's God is the god of his own creation and not the true God. For Blake, Satan's deception *is his claim to be God as he assumes power; the god within falls into deathly sleep of spiritual amnesia so Satan can make havoc of Job's world* (p. 186).

Blake, according to Raine (1971), places the time that the legend of Job was written sometime between 800-300 B.C. Mitchell agrees with these dates in part, but both he and Blake state that the legend was already old long before this time.

This study includes some of Blake's very moving images of Job's struggle with God. These and some of the poetry of Job may help clarify the archetypal aspects of Job as victim. The images were chosen from paintings about the story of Job as

Blake saw them. Raine edits and interprets the images, not so much as illustrations of the Bible, but as Blake's visions of man's spiritual drama. He felt the true God was the God within.

The following images were copied from ARAS, San Francisco C. G Jung Institute, 1990. The observations are made by Kathleen Raine (1971).

Image #1

Observations

Image #1 is of Job's family at evening prayers. Job and his wife are sitting under a tree and the children are kneeling. Musical instruments hang on the tree and the parents have books in their laps. Sheep are grazing nearby. It is a peaceful scene. Blake thought that the books showed that Job lived by the letter, not necessarily by the spirit, of the law.

Image #2

Observations

Image #2 shows a very different scene. It displays Job smitten with boils from head to foot. Satan stands over the prostrate figure. It is a scene of desolation. Satan's right hand holds four arrows, indicating the death of Job's four senses: sight, hearing, taste, smell. Job's wife is kneeling, head in hands, at his feet.

Image #3

Observations

Image #3 shows Job when his three friends come first to comfort him and then to accuse him for saying that God is unjust. Job's wife is kneeling behind him; he is sitting, weary and dejected.

Image #4

Observations

Image #4 shows Job as he realizes more fully the injustice of his situation. He says, "Let the day perish wherein I was born." After seven days of passive acceptance, he begins to question the justice of his situation. His wife is kneeling at his right side and his three friends are kneeling at his left. This is the scene of the state of Job's Revelation.

Image #5

Observations

Image #5 shows Blake's representation of God answering Job through the power and movement of the whirlwind. His friends are crouched down, while Job and his wife face God with their heads up and hands folded. God, with flowing hair and beard and arms outstretched, is Jesus, the Divine imagination, and the Forgiveness of Sins: (this is the only God whom Blake recognizes).

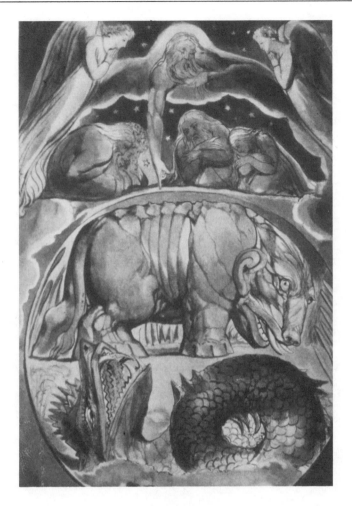

Image #6

Observation

Image #6 is Blake's vision of the universe as the four-fold soul of man: the flesh, the brain, the heart, and the imagination. Job, his wife, and his friends are represented as the world of flesh and are enclosed within a thick cloud barrier. Above is Apollo, the sun god, representing intellect. Diana, the moon goddess, guides the dragons of passions in the night. Highest of all are the angels of imagination separated by only a thin line of clouds. In the center is God kneeling, protecting the brain and heart. In the bottom frame is the body of Leviathan of nature in the Sea of Time and Space. Below him is the worm of death, coiled around a corpse.

Image #7

Observations

In Image #7, God is casting Satan into the flames of annihilation and Job and his wife are separated from their friends.

Image #8

Observations

Image #8 shows Job praying for the forgiveness of his friends who are kneeling behind him. There is an arch of sun and an arc of clouds. Blake felt that Job's body defined a cross and that his prayer was inward, since he faced inward.

Image #9

Observations

Image #9 is the final illustration. It shows Job reunited with his family. Here they are playing their musical instruments, which were hanging in the tree in the first illustration. They are all standing together in celebration, making joyful music. The moon and sun are shown. Sheep and lambs are in the foreground. This is where Job acknowledges his daughters and gives them the names of Poetry, Music, and Painting. Blake calls this the ninth stage in the state of New Life.

Mitchell (1987) pictures Job as being afraid of God, and worried about making a mistake. His first speech says, "My worst fears have happened; my nightmares have come to life. Anguish camps in my heart" (p. 14). Job is not whole; he must hurtle to the bottom of despair before he can begin to stand up for himself. He maintains throughout the poem that *suffering comes from God; I am innocent and therefore God is unjust* (p. 64).

Mitchell states that even Job's friends are afraid of contact with him and recycle over and over the same arguments against him. Job repeats the old question, "Why me?" There is no answer because it is the wrong question. Job suffers his own pain and that of all the poor and despised. He never stops loving God, but he is outraged by Him. Mitchell says that when Job was finally able to stand before God as a prince, he then was carried into the eye of the whirlwind. God will not hear Job, but Job will see God.

Job was finally able to accept or submit to the victimization of the ego, as painful as it was. He faced evil and looked straight into the vast wonder of it with love. Mitchell sees this as surrender, the whole-hearted giving up of one's self.

In complete surrender, Job is able to see the light and know that suffering and joy come like a brief reflection. Mitchell continues by stating that the theme of the book is spiritual transformation. In the beginning there was a family, drowsing; at the end, the world is transformed and the family is fully awake. The daughters are named and given equality with the sons. The center of the story has shifted from righteousness to beauty and inner peace. Now the victim, Job, has learned to submit. When Job is healed, death comes peacefully and lovingly.

Jung's Answer to Job

Jung (1952) explains that when we deal with religious concepts, *we are dealing with psychic facts which logic can overlook but not eliminate...statements of the soul are about realities that transcend consciousness* (pp. 17-18). They are based on numinous archetypes, so we must allow for some subjectivity. He calls the Book of Job a landmark of divine drama. He pictures Yahweh amorally with both loving kindness and cruelty, creative power and destructiveness. He feels that divine darkness was unveiled in the Book of Job and this gives us a certain experience of God. Jung says that we need to submit to the violence of life and be affected by it in order to transform the blindness of this phenomenon. Jung wants to know why and to what purpose Job was wounded. Job was aware of the unity of God, but he could not see the evil of Yahweh. Ironically, Yahweh is both persecutor and helper .

Jung insists that God needs humanity and humanity needs God. He is everything in totality—total justice and its total opposite. Jung suggests that it is up to humanity to make God more conscious. Job is the first person to force God to reveal his true nature, but God turns the tables on Job and blames him for what he himself does. Yahweh is a phenomenon, as Job says, not a person. Still, Yahweh's dual nature is revealed by Job. He becomes the one with whom both Satan and God experiment to find reasons why he disobeys and seeks wisdom. Jung also speaks of Sophia as the omnipotent feminine partner of God who has been forgotten in heaven and is still needed to maintain the balance of evil and good on earth.

Jung continues with more metaphysical material from the book of Revelations. For example, he asserts that God needs humanity for his own transformation, just as Job needs God for his wholeness and wisdom. He reminds individuals that Heaven is masculine but that Earth is feminine nourisher. It is up to individuals to be more conscious of the immense power now in their hands and to temper their wills with the spirit of love and wisdom. Job made the first step in humanity's climb up to a higher plane of consciousness without succumbing to passive victimization. Jung ends his study by saying that God is not only to be loved but also to be feared. The psyche is real and in the unconscious is an archetype of wholeness and healing, if one can hold the opposites together long enough to bear the pain of suffering and joy together.

Nagel (1954) comments on Jung's answer to Job by stating that the image of God is not static. Conscious man has a part to play in its development. It is not just man's answer but God's as well. She says that even an illumined human being remains that which he is. This is in contrast to him who dwells within—deep as earth and spacious as sky (God).

Jung's words about the archetype of healing being present in the unconscious has been shown by examples and proven to be true at different times and places, both presently and in the past. In this study of victimization, much effort is extended in showing that victim and victimizer are real and a part of our collective world. For healing to be possible, humans must understand and take more responsibility for finding out more about this phenomenon—and especially learn to recognize the victim, both in the outside world and within each of us. If each person, including children, can become as responsible as possible, then some of the present epidemic of child abuse and violence will come closer to consciousness, thus enabling better ways of treatment to be found.

Other Hero Victims

Fortunately, besides universal figures such as Job, there are many other examples of humans who have already proven, or are now proving, the power of archetype hero martyr or victim. Victor Frankl, for example, is one person who was able to make a difference in the lives of many people interned in a prison camp during World War II. He also helped to change the collective world as well. Frankl's book (1969) describes the hardships endured in the camp. More importantly, it shows how even a few martyrs can make a difference in the collective world when they are able to contain even a small part of evil until other, more unconscious, individuals can perceive the necessity of change within themselves and in society as a whole. Then, very pronounced changes can, and do, take place in the world generally. For example, when Frankl was able to objectify, even to a small degree, the degradation suffered by the prisoners under very cruel Nazi guards, he was able not only to help his fellow prisoners but also to perceive that the guards themselves were actually victims as well—victims of an unjust system and an unreal power that could change their lives from guards to prisoners at any overseer's whim.

Mother Teresa is another example of hero-martyr. She is moved by a deep responsible archetype that inwardly leads her to help all people without bitterness, and to do so with a great deal of joy. There must be a numinous inner power within her psyche that gets replenished over and over again. Even though she is a very old woman now, and not at all well physically, she continues to have the strength and will to improve the lives of many people—men, women, and children. Some individuals may call her a victim or a martyr: in one way she is hero-victim. However, no one can deny that she has remarkable influence on the rich and the poor, on people of all races and creeds. When she heals only a few victims it does make a difference in the individual community and collective unconscious in general.

Summary

This chapter discusses Job as universal victim, containing the suffering of all humans. Many writers see this story as a fore-runner to the life of Jesus, as Christian hero martyr. Job's story is essential to this study as an example of how collective unconscious and archetypes do exist and have from the beginning of time. It gives a powerful example of how consciousness of man and God can evolve.

V. CASE STUDIES

CASE STUDY #1 - JOHN

Boy - Age 9 - Victim from Birth.

In Chapter IV an example of victim and archetype was described in terms of myth and history. As an illustration, the universal story of Job was related, as a prelude, to some of the more collective problems that connect to modern victimization and violence. Special attention now needs to focus on the inner and outer child. One introduction to this area is through telling the stories of four different victimized children. These children all suffered deep pain within their families as scapegoat or unconscious victim. Each was treated with sandplay therapy which leads to soul healing from deeper suffering of an archetypal fate and from personal and collective trauma.

Sandplay is a unique therapeutic method and works especially well for children who have been made victim from very traumatic outer or inner events. By playing creatively in an especially built sand tray, both children and adults are given a chance to express themselves in images or symbols. Although the path of each individual is different, each person follows the three stages of development that Dora Kalff (1980) called (1) the vegetative and animal phase, (2) the fighting or confronting phase, and (3) the phase of adaption to the collective. Eric Neumann (1973) amplifies and extends these stages of child development.

Estelle Weinrib (1983) states that Sandplay stages evolve out of a nonverbal, nonrational, and autonomous process, and that it offers evidence of Neumann's theory that early development of the personality is an essentially unconscious, archetypally determined process.

In the case of John, age nine, Sandplay offered a safe place to directly enter into his inner world of feeling, with some separation from the archetype of *all good* mother. As a victim from a very traumatic birth process, he either inherited or developed a matriarchal split in his then weak ego. Sandplay therapy gave him a way of repairing his *too perfect biological mother image* and thereby a chance to develop a healthier acceptance of a more human mother. His daily experiences could then become more balanced by his clearer acceptance of both the good and bad or the dark and light aspects of everyday living. In other words, this case study shows how a young boy, born as victim, was able to heal his archetypal birth trauma through sandplay therapy.

John's Story

John's mother was seriously ill during much of her pregnancy with this child and was in a coma at the time of his birth. She died a few months after he was born, and John was cared for by his father and paternal grandparents for the first four years of his life, at which time his father remarried. Those early three to four years of this boy's life were very chaotic and difficult for all of the family, according to John's father. In addition to physically caring for both the child and his mother, there was the extra burden of coping with huge medical expenses. John worked with a male therapist for several years and then was referred to me for more maternal nourishing, as he was continuing to have great trouble accepting his step-mother even after four years.

Everyone in the family, including the paternal grandmother, had tried hard to nurture John; yet, he seemed unable to accept love from family members or teachers. The boy was referred to me for therapy in the hope that by working with a woman, and in sandplay, he would be able to open up more to his stepmother so that a real family could be created. Both parents and grandparents sought healing for John and for more harmony within the family.

Through the first four years of John's life, all of his family were in therapy part of the time. This continued, to some extent, after his father remarried. John spent time in various creative nurseries and private schools from age two to eight. Most of the adults in his life during those years seemed to agree that he was a very bright little boy, and that he could even be loving at times. However, reports showed that much of the time John was quite wild and unmanageable. John himself told me very soon after he started working with me that I could not possibly imagine how wild he really was. It seems that at school he spent much time running around, up and down the halls, or screaming and trying to involve other children in outrageous behavior. Teachers, counselors, and parents tried hard to tame this child's outbursts, apparently, with much love and understanding. John had been named *stone-heart* by one of his teachers, and his stepmother told me that this was an apt description. He had been kept on very heavy doses of hyper-activity suppressors for most of his life before he came to me for therapy.

Early Work in Sandplay Therapy

For some almost mysterious reason, John brought nothing but great love to me, even in his first few sessions. He was affectionate, and was soon making creative sand pictures. He accepted me as therapist, was confidant immediately, and ready to work positively. From the beginning of our sessions, he told me what he called *big secrets*. Our transference and counter-transference throughout our many sessions was strong and mutually affectionate. Apparently, John felt safe relating to me. This therapist shows great affection for children, generally, and, for some reason, John's great need for giving and receiving love touched my deeper psyche. It was as though John had been looking for a nourishing mother, and felt too guilty or disloyal to his image of blood mother to show any love to his stepmother. The goal of therapy for John was to help this boy transfer some of his positive feelings for his therapist back to his stepmother.

This affectionate transference did not stop the many stormy and painful sessions in which John would be angry internally and have trouble expressing it verbally and directly. He was able to verbalize quite clearly his hostility towards his stepmother and, sometimes, even his father. He disagreed very strongly with their methods of isolating him for punishment, but admitted he could not tell them directly. Instead, he pretended to enjoy this quiet time in his room or he would *act out* his anger by destroying something or refusing to talk to them.

One of my early suggestions to John's parents was that they ask their physician to reduce the dosage of John's medication. The physician agreed, and in only a few months, John was able to tolerate school for a full day without any medication. Home life continued to be somewhat hectic and chaotic during these first few months of therapy. I gave the parents suggestions for better ways of communicating with John. Both his father and stepmother were currently in therapy, sometimes individually and sometimes together; so my main work was always with John, observing and assessing his developmental process in sandplay.

This creative play therapy was a natural for this boy, and he never tired of creating his beautiful and interesting scenes. In most sessions he would finish his scene before he talked to me quite openly about school, his family, and himself. He worked fast, but never erratically, and was never satisfied until the complete picture was finished. Sometimes he did talk during the creation of his pictures, but this did not happen often. Occasionally, he would finish a scene early and would be delighted just to play with the sand in a second tray; sometimes we made lemonade from fresh lemons picked from my tree. He seemed to know his limitations about sugar and its effect on his hyperactivity; so he was able to judge for himself the amount of sugar he could tolerate. These few shared minutes outside of sandplay seemed very helpful to John.

Sandplay Therapy, Six Months to Two Years

After about six months of working in sandplay therapy, John was not only taller but much healthier. No longer taking medication, he was able to tolerate regular group sports and activities in a regular classroom. He still had some problems getting along with other children, and his father felt he had few, if any, friends his own age. We were now able to talk rather freely about this, and John stated that he was aware of this and assured me he was improving and that he was trying to be more aware of other people's feelings. Once in a while I would play an outdoor game with him, but it seemed that he preferred competitive games that he could play by himself. However, he always wanted me to be with him and watch what he was doing.

John had been working with me in sandplay for just over six months, when he began to express much confusion surrounding his background, his blood mother, and his grandparents. He tried to be open about these matters, and was able to listen more quietly when I tried to answer some of his questions. The most difficult work for John at this time was admitting he was angry and then working it out cooperatively. Many times he would be angry over something, but would refuse to say what until he finally did something outrageous; then his parents felt they were forced to punish him. Yet, these tactics did not work either.

John had been in therapy for almost six months before he was finally able to express conscious anger towards me. I had spent some of his regular therapy hour with his father. Although he said nothing to me at that time, I felt his outrage. He had slipped out to my newly planted front lawn and made several deep footprints. When I became more conscious of his message, I was able to explain to John, in a non-threatening way, that I would not care any less for him if he made a mistake. I added that I thought he would be happier if he could admit that it was he who had made the prints and then he could let go of his guilt.

I suggested that he had a right to be angry and that I hoped after this he could let me know more clearly about his angry feelings towards his family, friends, or me. Somehow my spontaneous way worked. It empowered this boy in a human, inner way that was satisfying for both of us.

Perhaps a more formal approach to interpretation and assessment could have been used with John. I am not sure. But after this incident, he was able to tell me, and his father, his teacher, classmates, and his stepmother about some of his difficulties, frustrations, and anger.

Starting out in almost complete chaos, John, in his sandplay therapy, became more conscious of both his inner unexpressed anger and his victimization. He was then able to make calm, more peaceful adjustment to his home, community, and school. There is still need for more work on clearer communication between John and his parents. But this will no doubt happen in a more cooperative atmosphere.

Sandplay Images

John's sand picture images give a clear picture of his inner psyche, and to some degree, of his outer conscious feelings and ego adjustments as well. His images trace a spiralling movement from chaos or vegetative stage to the conflicting fighting stage process, and finally to his own healing of self. The deepest development in John's psyche and ego appeared to come from his clear reconnection to his transcendent Self. As a baby and young child, he no doubt connected to an all perfect, archetypal good Mother, rather than relating to a true human, nourishing mother. Since there was no actual biological mother to relate to, or to separate from, his father and his paternal grandmother became the nourishing surrogate parents. This made John a victim from birth.

However, with the positive support from his father and paternal grandparents, and later from a stepmother and a loving therapist, he was able to develop a strong ego fairly early. His ego may not have been too well balanced or centered in his early years, but it did continue to move towards John's own unique, centered self. Certainly he became more accepting of his own unique fate and journey.

John's many sand tray creations over his two years of therapy clarify some of the mystery of healing that takes place in sandplay therapy, particularly for the victim. This process helps one to live in his or her outer world as well as in the deeper inner world, not without conflict, but with some grace and happiness, and with a deep connection to the inner child. This continues to give both the child and the adult a deep feeling of acceptance or being in relation to his or her own special journey and fate.

Image #1

John's first image shows disorganization, with figures crowded together somewhat chaotically. He puts in airplanes and army equipment, with one red pterodactyl and two flags of identity. It is a picture of much hidden anger. His choice of red (the color of passion) and a prehistoric animal, indicates that his negative instincts were still deeply unconscious.

Image #2

Image #2 shows many buildings, houses, castles, and animals all scattered about. This picture is disorganized and very crowded, too. One very positive figure is the bird and tree or spirit and earth. His next few pictures are of animals, houses, and people, and these sand images are much more human and differentiated.

Image #3

The next 12 sand pictures show remarkable changes in John's psyche. I show only three since the purpose of this study is not to divulge complete case studies but rather to trace the evolving pattern of a child's inner and outer psyche development. John moves from chaos to a deep relationship to the earth and sky and especially to his individual self, and thus to healing. The first image shown here is of a spiral cave, showing how water can flow in and out. Animals of many varieties are in all his pictures. The most important ones in this series show a healthy conflict in his world. Those relating to the positive aspects of motherhood are represented by the elephant and bear.

More negative ones are the rhinoceros and possibly the inert standing camel and mouse. Other figures, some of rebirth and change, are the magic emerald mushroom, large tree, with its changing position, and the bird.

Image #4

The volcanos shown in both Images #4 and #5 are no doubt necessary, and John speaks of the possible danger of this. He indicates, however, that the mirror in #5 gives the good animals a light for their journey.

Image #5

The next series of pictures shows what is often referred to in Jungian terms as the emergence of the Self and Rebirth. John shows this by his choice of animals—primarily butterfly, snake, turtle, and duck (all old mythological figures of long life and change). The arrangement of the lakes, mandala shapes, birth of Christ scene, four angels around the bear, and the wonderful centering of his pictures are all a part of this phase of his development.

During this series of rebirth scenes, John also produced his own creation myth. It appears below in his exact words. Image #6 shows his scene.

The Making of Japan Land

"First came the big tree, right in the center of the world. (They do not know how, but they have proved it, since from the old parts of this tree new trees have grown). A very beautiful green mushroom is always found in front of this special tree, and it is magical. All the elves and dwarfs live there, also. Next came the gods - lots of them - the Laughing Buddha, the dark one, and the boy-face, along with other child gods. Then there was a small village, and it needed light; so a light came on. (Here he literally went over and turned on a light). A few other small houses were added, and then more trees grew from the big one. A big temple was built there, also. Next came the animals; only they were god animals, also, and very special, like the king lion and the special healing snake, who also was worshiped. There was a white god, like Pegasus, and there was a stand for the great lion, and this still remains. Next there were two dark and very tall candy dancing gods, and they threw candy and food everywhere; so there was candy and food for everybody. There was a small, but deep lake, for the fish. It was magical, as were the fish and water.

SO THIS IS THE LAND OF FULLY PEACE AND HAPPINESS NOW.

Image #6

In Image #6, the laughing Buddha and the boy-faced, special child occupy prominent places. The special lion is in front of the village. The big tree is hard to see, but it is in the center of his picture; with the bird high on some branches and the magic mushroom on the ground. God children and the candy, or food, are throughout the picture. The two dancing figures are across from each other in the back part of the tray. Needless to say, watching this boy produce his sand picture and relate it to me verbally was a very moving and numinous experience for both of us.

Image #7

Image #7 shows two lakes as the waters of life and the emergence of the Self. This is another numinous experience, which occurs with very deep inner feeling, for both the child and the therapist. This, and the image following, were produced several months after John's creation myth image. When a child produces emergence and rebirth sand pictures, he or she may not always be completely conscious of what is happening, but the therapist needs to be completely aware. The child is usually also aware that something different is happening inside himself or herself. He or she often shows a change in outer behavior as well, even though it may not have been talked about verbally or interpreted too objectively.

Image #8

Image #8 is the birth of the savior child. It was created in the month of April. When such an image follows an emergence scene like the previous one (#7), it is considered a Rebirth and gives a new dimension to the Self emergence theme. As a type of ritual, John put a burned-down shell-like candle in the center of his picture and lit it at the completion of his creation.

Image #9

Images #9 and #10 both show John's need to express outwardly his inner anger. Number nine is an intricate fighting scene with a lone soldier on the bridge. John tells me he is holding the two sides in balance and the Indians are protecting their own land and homes.

Image #10

Image #10 is somewhat unusual for a child of age 9. However, John seems to know exactly what he needs to do. He lines the figures in a kind of semi-circle across the sand tray and places a white stand with the circular, clear ball on top. Next, he puts a large, dark doll facing the round ball and says he is looking right at the magical ball. John was clearly and bravely confronting the dark shadow, and his ego was strong enough to do this now.

Image #11

Images #11 and #12 seem to amplify the last two. They show the devil or shadow figure being contained by knight soldiers. His favorite bear is in the center of each picture; the bear is alone in #11 and surrounded by four angels in #12. Many of his favorite animals such as the turtle, fish, the blue horse and whales are in both pictures. John says the devil is being kept in check by the knights so he cannot harm the others.

Image #12

Image #12, although very similar to #11, shows some differences that are significant. The turtle has a central place in #12, and no doubt refers back once more to his earlier deep-seated feelings of abandonment. This time the turtle is trudging forward toward the little boat and the special boy. This is the first time he has chosen the laughing Buddha who seems to bring more joy into his personal and family life.

Image #13

This picture shows another, clearer image of the emergence of the Self. John represents this numinous experience by placing his favorite bear in the center of the tray with four trees making a full circle (mandala or a circle within a square). In each of the outside four corners are villages, animals of all kinds, and angels. His favorite girl and boy are in the right center edge of the tray. The magic healing mushroom is between them. The turtle and his favorite junket boat are in the water, encircling the mandala and separating the two lands. This true mandala, or quarternity (four trees inside a circle or a circle inside the rectangular, four-sided sand tray), is often considered by Jungians as wholeness or individuation. It is more often related to adults rather than to children, but in this therapist's practice this deep centering has happened with children as well.

Image #14

John calls his last picture *Earth and Heaven* and represents it by placing a small ladder in the center of the sand tray. First, he puts many of his favorite figures in the sand tray itself, and then he places different ones on each step of the ladder. For

John to say "this is earth and heaven" seemed quite natural at this time. He had used similar terms before. He seems to feel just as much at ease in relating symbols to objects. He calls the round crystal *God* and then later says *It* made the sun move. In any case, at this point in therapy, I felt very sure of John's inner centering and recognized a stronger outer ego as well.

There is no way to share this case study in depth without seeing all of his images and following the process as it spiralled from chaos to confronting, to adjusting to the collective. Anyone interested in obtaining permission to see the full case study can do so at the C.G. Jung Institute, San Francisco.

C.G. Jung (1961) and others have said that deep in the unconscious there is a tendency for the psyche to heal itself. This is my firm belief and experience has verified this in the lives of many children and adults who have worked with me in sandplay therapy. Many therapists, including Neumann (1973), stress the need of very early mother-child unity. Because of the early birth-trauma for John, he did not have this needed mother connection in his early years. However, I do agree that self is present at birth and that John inherited strong instinctual self-preservation traits from the beginning. In sandplay therapy, he had a chance to reconstruct a new mother-child unity in order to reconstruct Self and self.

Sandplay offered a safe place for John to directly enter into his own world of feelings and transpersonal experiences in order to heal the matriarchal split. It gave him a way to repair his mother-image of archetypal *all-good, perfect mother* and to relate to a more human acceptance of life balanced by both good and bad aspects. He was fortunate to have a good patriarchal model and loving grandparents to help him separate and move into the outside world more creatively. During his two years with me in sandplay therapy, John created his own rites of passage through the maze of producing his intricate sand pictures. Creative play was his tool; the therapist, his sheltered place, the symbolic miniatures and sand, his vessel of passage.

Even though John talked very little directly about his sand pictures, he communicated many of his fears, joys, and secrets with me, both outwardly and inwardly. Much more communication is needed between his parents and him, but, as John becomes more and more centered and his ego more integrated, this outward healing will be more complete.

Summary

John and his family have suffered. They are all victims in one sense. Each has to find his or her right journey or true fate. John worked with and experienced many symbols and images. He shared some dreams and related these to some parts of his outer world. He, no doubt, will spiral back and forth between joy and sorrow, depending partly on whatever outer experiences he encounters. However, he has begun to learn about balancing the opposites of good and bad in life and accepting both from time to time.

Of all the symbols John chose for his sand pictures, his most favorite ones were the tree, the bear, and the magic mushroom. The fact that the mushroom replica was green, or emerald, makes it doubly healing. That the emerald is considered the most precious of stones, adds to its mystery and numinosity. In many myths the tree is both earth and spirit, or father sky and mother earth. It is also a symbol of heaven and earth. Laurens van der Post has said many times that Jacob's image of the ladder up to heaven, as related in the Bible, is every person's connection to the Higher Self and to each other, with angels being the connecting link. John shows in his last picture that he has found his own connecting links and symbols to life, inwardly and outwardly.

John's case study is related to this clinician's study in the following ways. One, victimization is a part of, and the responsibility of, every person. John took on much of his own burden by searching and finding his own center and self. Two, he was able to make direct contact and even confront the moving symbols that his unconscious led him to choose in his sandplay therapy sessions. With his therapy work and the support of loving parents and grandparents, he did humanize some of the archetypes, especially the *too perfect mother imago* that possessed his early life, thus transforming his victimization to more creative living.

CASE STUDY #2 - SUZZI

Girl - age 14 - Victim of Attempted Suicide

Case Study #2 is about a girl, age 14, whom we call Suzzi. She came to me for help after having previously attempted suicide. This therapist worked with Suzzi 14 years ago, using sandplay as the primary technique of analysis. Sandplay works especially well for children who are victims either of traumatic outer or inner events. If the therapy can continue long enough for the individual to move through a clear process with the mentor, healing takes place.

When Suzzi first appeared at my office, she was a very sad child, seeming younger than her actual age. She came into the therapy room with head bent and shuffled along rather than walking straight and tall.

Sandplay Sessions

Suzzi seemed more alert when she saw the sand trays, miniatures, and toys in the room. In fact, she seemed at ease when I suggested that she get acquainted with the many figures, toys, and symbols while I talked to her parents in another room. She could feel free to place as many of the figurines as she wished in one or the other of the two trays, either the dry one or the one to which she could add water.

Ordinarily, a child or a teenager does not do a sand picture without the therapist, but it seemed right this time and the parents and I were close by in the next room. Nevertheless, I was somewhat surprised when I returned to discover Suzzi's first sand picture, a community full of activity. There was much movement and the whole picture denoted a busy life, in contrast to the outer ego that Suzzi was showing.

Image #1

Suzzi chose a large train station and placed it on the far west or left side of the sand tray, with at least 20 tiny figures of people standing outside the station. She put one man alone on a single bench. On the southern or bottom part of the tray, she fenced in groups of cows, pigs, and other animals, with people feeding them. On the eastern or right side of the tray, she placed two houses. One is unfinished and people are working on it and in the fields nearby. In the center of her picture, Suzzi placed a church, and next to it another unfinished house. She put a small house with a water wheel in the northwest or top left corner of the tray and this completed her picture. The intricacy and beauty and movement of Suzzi's first sand picture helped me to intuit more about her inner psyche at that time.

At her next session Suzzi was able to verbalize more readily and told me about a boy she liked but was unable to handle their friendship, especially since one of her younger brothers always tried to monopolize her friend's attention. I asked her if she had talked to her father about helping her with this problem. Apparently, Suzzi had tried but felt that her dad did not understand. Suzzi also told me that the girls she wanted to be friends with told her she acts too young and too shy. Suzzi continued telling me she was sure her parents liked the younger children better than her and that one brother was very talented in art, and one sister outshadowed her as a student

As the sessions continued, Suzzi also shared the fact that she missed the city life of their previous home; she was not happy in her present environment, a small town. She said she had no friends or groups she could join. For example, she had enjoyed dramatics in the city and missed this very much presently. After this Suzzi made several sand scenes and, one day, painted a very vivid picture of herself, using heavy red paint on her face and hands.

Suzzi's Image of Herself

Suzzi declared that the picture was ugly. However, she seemed pleased with it as well, as she placed a ribbon in the figure's hair. It is clearly a sad, immature drawing for a girl of fourteen, but one in which she did depict her own insecure feelings of self. Her painting depicts an unsmiling, not-quite-human face with arms and hands indistinguishable. She chose not to show the lower part of the body.

Unfortunately, Suzzi's parents decided it was necessary to break off therapy before too many more sessions, saying they could not afford it because of their large family. I was sad but also grateful that, even though Suzzi had been in therapy for only a few months, she had progressed rapidly and seemed much happier about both her home and school life.

Suzzi's last sand picture was in the form of a very important ritual. She went directly to the sand tray that particular day and, with only a few words, started her sand picture.

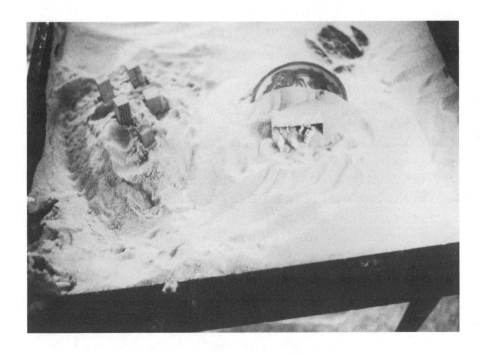

Imgage #2 — Death and Rebirth

This is a realistic picture about death and burial, and the process of reincarnation that often occurs when one wants to live, not die. It is like a reenactment of Suzzi's own attempted suicide. The following describes the scene just as Suzzi related it.

First, Suzzi asked if I had some miniature figures she could use as grave stones. I found some wooden posts, that looked like blocks, and she liked them. She then very carefully dug graves in the sand and buried the figures of people in these holes, and then very slowly covered each grave with sand; she then indented the sand in front of each headstone to show exactly where the graves were. All the graves are on a higher mound of earth located in the lower west corner of the tray.

Next, Suzzi did something rather unusual. She asked if she might use my one lovely china plate, covered with intricate gold-plated dragons. This plate is rarely ever used in the sand. She half-buried the plate to the right of the graves, and then turned the exposed part of the figure with her hand so that the gold designs caught the sunlight and gleamed brightly. Suzzi turned the plate back and forth, saying that this action symbolized the *resurrection*, which had the power to bring those buried on the hill back to life. Watching the turning of the plate, and the brilliant light was a powerful and hypnotizing experience for both of us. The plate seemed to take on the strength and numinosity of the sun, a symbol often used for God, both by primitives and in more modern cultures as well.

Next, Suzzi placed the figures of a man and a woman in the sand at the top west or left corner and called them a *mother* and a *father* who were looking for their lost child. She moved the figures over to the gold plate deeper in the sand, and then placed the figures of some workers in front of the buried plate and showed them digging in the sand. Next, Suzzi dug a water hole in the sand to the back and east of where the workmen were digging. She then very quietly and slowly uncovered the buried plate and moved it around again to catch the light. As she did this, she uncovered some of the buried people as well. One of these figures was a little girl.

"When the workmen find the plate, they find the lost child as well," Suzzi said. Having had long experience working with children, this therapist was not too surprised when she explained quite rationally that the plate has the power of resurrection or rebirth. She went on to say that when it is found, most of the people on the hill come back to life, and that the mother and father are happy to see the child again.

Suzzi had tried to kill herself. She had previously shared with me some of her feelings about why she had taken the pills. Now she revealed that she really did not want to die but was willing to take the chance in order to get her parents to notice her more. She told me there had seemed little to live for. However, when she brought the little girl back to life in the sand, something happened to her, and neither of us found the words to talk about her experience. Instead, we shared internally, not verbally. We did talk some about death and rebirth and Suzzi just smiled in a lovely, new, open way.

How the sand, the symbols, and the sacred and protected place, along with the patient and the therapist, all work together for healing is still a mystery. However, there is an autonomous, inner pulling towards healing for both children and adults when the situation is right. If the environment is conducive and the individual is able to suffer and submit to the ordeal until self or the center is experienced, it does happen and healing takes place.

Suzzi needed to get back to her undifferentiated instincts in order to find what she truly wants to follow as her fate for living. She has to wait and listen and even love her own self before she can find her true journey. The attempted suicide, therefore, was a part of her battle to be understood and loved by others.

However, this alone is not enough; Suzzi had to understand her own self more deeply. Producing the sand scenes in the presence of a trusted *other* helped her imagine who she really was. She found that love of life and her own creativity were inside her own psyche. Now she can love herself and move from friendship inside to love for others outside. Instead of retreating and staying the passive victim, she can move closer to her own *hero self*.

The intricacy and beauty of Suzzi's first sand picture shows great trust and the need to be open. This picture indicates something of her former life in the city; that she is trying to integrate the two kinds of life. In a later session, when she painted a picture of herself, she depicted her own feelings of her present self. At this point, she was able to clarify some of the pain she suffered internally, but was unable to communicate it to her family or friends.

Suzzi's last picture of her own resurrection was the focal point of her healing process. The production of the scene, and the sharing later, opened the door to transformation of her self. She was brave and open when she created this picture. Even though longer therapy was indicated, Suzzi made great progress in the short term of her sandplay therapy. The harmony and centering of her own psyche moved deeper.

Epilogue

The family and Suzzi kept some contact with me for the next five years. At age 19, this young girl seemed strong inwardly and outwardly and on her own individual journey. She was no longer the passive victim, and apparently found her own individual creativity inside her psyche, which gave her the inner strength to take charge of her own self.

It was Suzzi's father who came to tell me that his daughter, at age 19, had reported him for child molestation. He had just spent two years in detention, and with supportive therapy, was now able to mend his own angry and wounded inner child. He was now reunited with the family in a more loving and caring way. By developing her inner strength, Suzzi had moved from passive victim to hero, and her personality was transformed. Suzzi's father said he had come to thank me and to tell me that his daughter had now forgiven him.

Summary

Considering the short time that Suzzi was working in sandplay, it does not seem unusual that she did not share verbally the full depth of her anger towards her father. Most children have a kind of deep loyalty towards their family and an innate need to keep family secrets. It is hard for children to believe that their parents can ever be wrong or imperfect. Suzzi needed to develop her own inner strength before consciously being able to admit her full inner pain.

This therapist was present and shared Suzzi's reenactment of her own death attempt and rebirth. Some persons may call it *acting out*, but it surely was real, painful, and joyous. Some transformation or renewal of her personality did occur and could be observed both outwardly and inwardly as she left the therapy room after her last session.

In retrospect, there was some *acting out* on the part of Suzzi during her sandplay therapy sessions. This therapist does not see this as a *splitting off*. Transformation and rebirth cannot be proved any more than archetypes can be proven. It is simply something that has to be experienced in a truly knowing way. This writer feels privileged that she was allowed to share Suzzi's rebirth experience.

CASE STUDY #3 - JACK

Boy - Age 13 - Victim as Family Scapegoat

Case Study #3 (Jack) age 13, was treated by this therapist over 20 years ago. He recently made contact as an adult. He is one of the children described in the book, *Symbols Come Alive in the Sand*, (1978).

In the book, Jack's story is related to a very old Malayan myth of a young boy who had to stop his daydreaming and go on a long and heroic journey to find the other half of himself. It is actually an archetypal story of the journey that many young men need to take in order to become whole or centered in their individual lives. The story clearly relates to Jack's journey.

Jack's Story

Jack was 13 years old when he was referred to me for therapy treatment. He had been studied and diagnosed many times and I was shown many very thick files telling about all his problems. No one, it seemed, had been able to help him. He had been in special classes most of his academic years. When Jack was introduced to me, he was in a public junior high school in the seventh grade and he was apparently leading a miserable life there and at home.

Jack was the youngest child in a family of four children. The two older ones were in college and a brother, about four years older than him, was still in high school. The father was a professional man and the mother was very active in community and church affairs. My suspicion of Jack's position in the family as scapegoat was soon verified. Jack himself was very open about how the family viewed him, as clumsy and inferior. He said his brother in high school beat him up a great deal and that his parents did not interfere. He was afraid of this brother, but said his older sister did help him when she was home.

Jack was also afraid of his peers, especially the older boys, and often ran home from school in fright during school hours. When he did manage to stay in his classes, he never participated, nor did he cause trouble. The teachers reported that he never participated in discussions and usually drew pictures much of the time. So the teachers just left him alone. Occasionally, a teacher would try to involve him but apparently with little success. When he came to me, I was given permission to work with him as often as necessary, so we started out by my seeing him three times each week.

Sandplay Sessions

Sandplay was a real relief to Jack, and he always made his scenes with much energy and noise. I had never, and have never since, had any child who could imitate war or violent sounds more vividly than he could. His airplane movements and noises were loud and realistic and so were his descriptions of land and sea fighting. Sometimes, he asked permission to cut off the heads of plastic soldiers and when I gently suggested that perhaps he could substitute other methods just as satisfying, he would take crayons or red paint and cover the figures in imaginary blood. He could easily sustain real, blood-curdling war noises for a half hour or more at a time. He made many battle scenes in the sand, and often chose small white Arabs against dark American soldiers. (This is quite interesting in view of the dreadful and actual war between the U.S. and the Iraqi Arabs in January, 1991—a possible connection from the collective)

Jack used colorful language to describe his scenes. Once he ordered one of the soldiers: "Get up you fool and fight!" He told me that the soldier is a coward. Psychoanalysts might call this *acting out*. In one sense it was, but in Jack's case, this was an important step, since he had been so fearful of life generally and, also, of his peers. Witnessing the unfolding of a child or adult's unconscious and seeing the balancing of his or her self is a different kind of therapy from naming or diagnosing the resistances only.

Unfortunately, Jack destroyed most of his early scenes, so I was unable to photograph them. Later, when his battles became less tense and more organized, he was happy to let me take the pictures. I will show three images of battle only, with a later one of a spiral, showing some resolutions of his many problems. Two very early drawings portray Jack's inner and outer life quite vividly. Image #1 depicts a somewhat chaotic battle scene; Images #2 and #3 show a desert battle and a water battle. One drawing shows him shooting his peers and one is a tracing of his own hand, bleeding from a snake bite. It includes a baby snake being squeezed inside the picture of the mother snake.

Jack was one of this therapist's first patients in sandplay therapy and he taught me a great deal. He was able to depict, in his sand pictures, the state of his own inner psyche in a clearer way than any assessment tests could have done. Obviously, he needed no more testing as his many, thick files testify. Interpreting was necessary but not until his inner self had time to help correct or balance the opposites. Jack was not ready for direct confrontation before his unconscious led him towards balance and away from a splitting-off from his psyche.

Sandplay Images and Drawings

Image #1: A Chaotic Battle

Unfortunately, Image #1 is not too clear and Jack kept changing it as the battle raged. Suffice to say that it is full of his favorite very small fighting figures, Arabs and Americans, and a great many war planes and tanks.

Image #2: Battle on Land

This second scene above is fought on land, in the desert. Most of the soldiers and equipment are camouflaged and half buried. Interestingly, they are fighting over the water stream that he placed in the center of the tray. Jack called this scene "The Battle of Hell in the Black Desert." He told me no one would win and he thought war was terrible. The desert indicates how his emotions have been choked off and that he needs to regain or win back the water of life to survive.

Later, he told me that he really liked to go to the desert with his family and find beautiful rocks and stones. These rocks seem to be symbols that he can keep in secret for himself alone.

The desert seems to describe for him his ugly outside life. Inside, he recognized that he had a more creative, inner, happier life symbolized by the stones and rocks. He also shared with me how rocks could be split and polished as true treasures.

Jack has a wonderful inside psyche that can be opened some day and polished and developed into a more centered life.

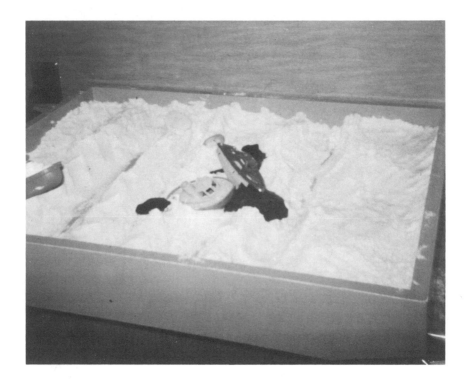

Image #3: Battle on the Sea

His water scene, above, is more peaceful, but it still depicts danger from the outside elements he told me about. Jack made what he called strong waves and put several boats near the center. This sea battle did help him open up more to his inner feelings in a more positive way, and he seemed to be less fearful after making this scene.

Image #4: A Spiral in the Sand

Jack's last sand picture was of a spiral of trucks and equipment. The spiral was like an "S" drawn backwards, and some of the trucks carried minerals and coal as well as army equipment for protection. This scene seemed to indicate that Jack was more into his masculine hero journey, but still recognized that he wanted more peace and harmony. The spiral helped him know his own center, or self, more consciously and to know that he could move from the dark mines into the outer world with less fear and more joy. It surely shows a beginning at least of integration of his early split ego or self.

In addition to Jack's work in sandplay, he drew and painted many pictures and made several clay pieces. His early pictures were of saber-toothed cats and of guns shooting at his peers. One was of a bomb placed inside his locker to blow up the school. I am including two realistic pictures, one of a large rattle snake squeezing and holding tight the baby snake inside. The snake is also biting a left hand that Jack had drawn by tracing his left hand and then showing drops of blood. The other picture shows him shooting a boy, whom Jack said was a peer enemy. These two pictures, which he drew in the early stages of his therapy show the tremendous progress Jack made in his own development from the beginning to his present stage.

Drawing A: Shooting at his Peers

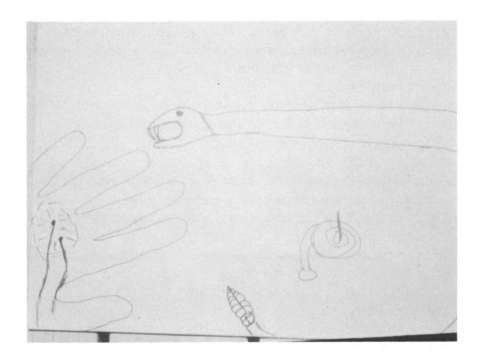

Drawing B: Snake Biting Jack's Hand

Family Secrets

Besides drawing and painting, Jack also liked to work with clay. One day he made a beautiful and intricately designed piece showing the entire family sitting at the dining room table. He even added a chandelier. When the entire piece was finished, Jack stood up as tall as he could and smashed the entire work of art into tiny bits. This therapist was startled and Jack was greatly surprised that he was not yelled at. He asked me whether I was angry, and I said, "no, only sad to see such a beautiful work destroyed"; now it was time for both of us to pick up the pieces and we did.

After this incident, Jack talked more about his family and repeated that he felt inferior to all of them. He said they picked on him, especially his next oldest brother. By smashing the family scene, much inner anger was obviously released. He seemed to see from his clay piece that his family was not at all in true harmony as his design shows. He simply needed to destroy that untrue image of a perfect family in order to release some of his own anger and guilt that was buried inside as a dreadful family secret.

After I knew Jack's family members better, I realized that his mother overprotected Jack. She was holding him too tightly and perhaps causing his psyche to bleed. This therapist was especially concerned about the older brother who seemed to delight in beating up Jack. However, when I attempted to approach the parents about the relationship between the two boys, they closed up completely and told me my work was with Jack alone and that they did not wish to be involved in whatever process the two of us were working on. They did express gratitude that he was doing so much better at home and in school, and said that he was beginning to make good friends in the neighborhood.

Several conferences were held with the parents and school personnel, and after two difficult but rewarding years of work with Jack in a safe and protected place, good reports were received. Jack was doing well in school now and was beginning to make many good friends; he said he was happier at home also, except for his older brother's treatment. When I pressed him for facts about how the brother acted with him, Jack, too, was vague and wanted to change the subject. Jack, like most children was unable to tell his therapist about sexual involvement with his older brother at this time. Unfortunately, children do feel both fear of and loyalty to their families. Children do tell their therapist about sexual molestation experiences, but not until deep trust has been established, and fear of family has been released. This therapist still feels some sadness that she was too inexperienced at the time when she was working with Jack to know how to confront his parents creatively about this matter. The time was 1970 and there was not much awareness and reporting of child molestation then. It is interesting, however, to remember that the parents had refused all discussion around the subject of the older brother at the time of Jack's early therapy. Yet, when Jack was accused of improper conduct with his own two small children, 20 years later, they made immediate contact to ask for my professional help. This therapist had kept some contact with the family for several years after the early work, and Jack had continued to do well on his own journey. He finished high school and then joined the Coast Guard, after which he managed his father's small cattle ranch. In all the occasional long letters from Jack's mother and cards from Jack, no one ever mentioned the older brother who had wounded this young man so deeply.

Summary and Further Evaluation

This case study is of a very sensitive and unique child who suffered and struggled very hard for healing. At the end of two years of analytical therapy work, he was able to recognize the opposites inside himself. From sandplay therapy he found soul healing and was able to feel much less the rejected victim.

According to one psychoanalyst's evaluation, Jack's first three sandplay pictures show *acting out,* and he states that the therapist did not perceive the true cause of Jack's rage. Looking back and clearly remembering this child as the therapist knew him at age 13, she knows now, and believes she did know then, that this boy's rage was ever present and real in the early productions of his sandplay dramas. He himself was a real part of those early war scenes and pictures when he symbolically wanted to blow up the school, cut off the heads of plastic soldiers, and shoot his peers. His rage penetrated the entire therapy room. The intensity of the thick air can still be felt in imagery. That he was close to explosion was evident; this therapist was glad that he chose the method of destroying the very creative fanciful and beautiful family scene, that he had produced in clay, to vent some of these dangerous, over-balanced emotions. She also believes that transformation did take place and that deep splitting-off would have been the result if too direct confrontation of his rage had been used as method of treatment.

Jack was one of the first children this therapist worked with in sandplay and she was quite relieved to see him gradually reduce some of his rage in creative sandplay. He had already been tested and diagnosed over and over again and was living under many negative labels long before he came to her office for treatment.

The material about Jack being accused of wrong treatment of his own two young children is added to give one more example of how victimization is carried on both within families and intergenerationally. It also shows once more that a strong connection happens in sandplay therapy, when there is time for the centering of the self to occur. Jack's actual legal case was dismissed, but with my advice and the support of others, he did agree to have more therapy.

CASE STUDY #4 - BOB

Boy - Age 6 - Victim of Abandonment in Infancy

The five case study summaries as related in this chapter give example and amplification of what this clinical psychologist sees as archetypal victimization. All of the four children became victim through no personal fault or trauma experienced consciously. Instead they each became victim from what appears to have come from overwhelming personal family events. Trauma events did occur in their lives, but these happenings were beyond the individual's control. In other words, both John and Bob were born as archetypal victims. Bob was born to professional parents who simply did not want to be parents at the time. They rejected or abandoned their child to so-called good parents in order to become free and continue their own individual lives as they perceived their journey to be. John was born from a biologically ill mother who never recovered. Suzzi and Jack were unwilling scapegoats in their families and at the mercy of unconscious parents; so they, too, became archetypal victims.

Inner and Outer Child

Before telling Bob's personal history, it is necessary to give some introductory observations about inner and outer child. When there is a lack of understanding of this important phenomena consciously, it can cause more negative violence to be left in the present collective consciousness. Fortunately, distinctions between inner and outer child are coming into focus in our modern Western world, probably because so much attention is being given to child abuse and to the victimization of all children. In literature and in clinical studies, it is frequently reported that the dysfunctional family is the cause of later addiction and violence in the individual. Both post-Jungians and post-Freudians are writing about the necessity of reclaiming the inner child.

The authentic Self, as Jung describes it, can be found only by understanding the wholeness in the child. Adult completeness can't be found within the realm of rationalism only. One must be able to descend to the realm of the unconscious. C. G. Jung did not write very much about childhood, but what he did write is most important to the modern child and adult. He spoke often of the inner child as the seed bearer of the Self: Jung (1932) wrote, *In every adult there lurks a child—an eternal child, something that is always becoming, is never completed, and calls for unceasing care, attention, and education. That is the part of the human persona which wants to develop and become whole* (p. 286).

Freud also expressed his deep interest in the child and said often that the job of therapy was the analysis of childhood.

Since early mother nurturing has become such an important issue in present therapies, it is important to say something about the archetype of mother. Jung (1927) talked about this aspect of the psyche many times. He (1932) included instincts that foster growth and fertility, maternal solicitude, sympathy, and wisdom as part of the archtype mother. At the same time, Jung also recognized the negative side of the mother clearly and called this archetype *the hidden, that which devours, and terrifies and often determines fate* (p. 187). He used Kali as an example.

Burkhauser-Oeri (1988) states that the mother archetype is concerned more with nature and instincts as images; father archetype is more concerned with spirit. The two represent the chief principles of all existence. They can form a harmonious union together or be opposites. Having close ties with the mother means being under the influence of the mother archetype. The result is destructive or creative depending on how a person relates to the internal image of the mother. The archetype image is not identical with the human mother.

Children live in a world of imagery much of the time from birth to the ages of four to five. If encouraged, quite young children will share their dream world and their world of fantasy with adults they trust. Fairy tale characters relate to the archetypes and children seem to understand this world easier, than most adults, unless the adult has a well-developed *inner child* that has not been too badly neglected.

Bob's Story

Sandplay therapy was the right tool for Bob since he was still carrying the archetypal seed and conscious pain from his unconscious parents when he was brought to me for therapy by his adopted parents at age six. He had been abandoned in infancy and thereafter carried the archetype of the innocent orphan until he was able to rebuild his own strong ego towards a more centered self by working in sandplay therapy.

Fortunately, Bob was adopted by very loving parents soon after birth, and they were able to recognize his inner feelings of rejection and need for therapy at an early age. Bob was in kindergarten at this time, a rather large child and somewhat awkward physically. The teachers complained of his aggressiveness with the other children, and he was having some learning problems as well. He had been adopted as an infant, and fairly soon thereafter a sister was born, so both children were close in age and grade, but very different in personality traits. She was petite, quite pretty, and popular, whereas he saw himself as not liked and inferior. Bob did have a deep sense of pride and rarely let anyone know how angry and hurt he was inside. Even though Bob had known about his adoption since he was very young, he was deeply hurt and felt humiliated when a very close friend at school told the other children that he was adopted. Unfortunately, the other children began to tease Bob about his adoption. The parents sought help at this time and this *tough little boy*, on the outside, and this therapist started our three years of work together.

Sandplay Images

One of Bob's very early pictures looked very much like a monster swimming in the water but connected to the land at one end.

Image #1

Image #1 is what this therapist calls a *monster*. Bob used all war equipment for the face; two jeeps for eyes; an army boat carrier for the nose; and a submarine for the mouth. This water image may have related to his own, pre-birth image, with no strong connection to his blood mother. Bob did very little talking during the making of his early pictures and he seemed fearful of the sand at first. However, after he faced his monster, or water archetype, he began to talk more and to make very interesting pictures.

Image #2

Bob flooded his sand trays over and over again (see Image #2 above). The above image was one of many. Bob built it in the form of a volcano, flooded it, and filled the picture with soldiers, some on horseback and some on foot. There was no true order to the picture. Therapy work with him was not easy since he continued to flood his trays for some time. The deep connection between us made me know that healing was taking place, and would continue, as he began to communicate more verbally and inwardly with his images in the sand.

Bob is one child who had no trouble giving names to his archetypal figures and he often chose clay figures that did represent old statues. Often he would point to a figure and say, "This is the green god, this the white god, and this the black god." He liked to melt paraffin and put coloring in it to represent some part of a scene or sand castle. He enjoyed painting and drawing pictures but had difficulty finishing them, and often destroyed them, still unfinished.

Besides his many flooding pictures, Bob went through a long series of fire pictures. They were very intense and at times needed to be contained. For example, at one time he wanted to burn the papers in my rather large trash can. So boundaries were needed and used from time to time.

Image #3

Image #3 is what Bob called a *ring of fire*. He asked for matches and quickly lit them, after placing them in a complete circle in the center of the tray. He put the other symbols, mostly war equipment, in the picture before making the fire image and also lit a candle in the center of the circle. He added one house, an umbrella, and a frog on the left side of the tray and placed two pieces of war equipment near the lighted matches. After completing this picture, he told me that his parents now trusted him with matches. Later, his parents explained to me that Bob, at age five, had started a large grass fire at the back of their lot and the fire department had to be summoned. During this time, Bob and I talked about creative and destructive fire, but words are unnecessary when transference and counter-transference are conscious with the therapist and even with the child to some degree. Also, Bob was now showing his very vulnerable and sweet inner side, and his sense of humor was beginning to show. In other words, some balance in his dark and light side was developing within his own self.

It was at this time, after ten months of therapy, that Bob, his parents, and the therapist decided it was to this boy's advantage to change schools for one year. He had a bad reputation in his present school; a year in a new environment would help to change his image. This worked out well, and Bob did very well in the new school. He made new friends and gained more confidence in himself. He decided to return to his old neighborhood and school for the following year.

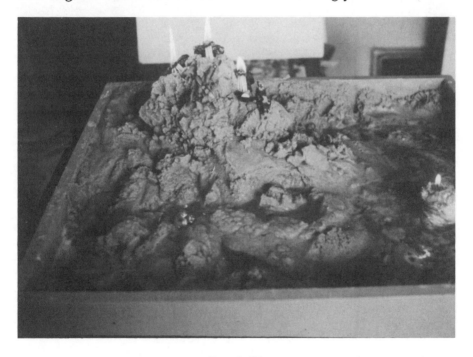

Image #4

Image #4 is another somewhat flooded picture. However, this one is organized and integrates fire with water. He added a small ceramic head of a man and put a lighted candle inside it. He put the soldiers on dry land and added a candle to the handmade castle on a hill in the left back corner. It appeared that both fire and flooding were now contained.

Image #5

This image shows a train moving on a track that Bob built very painstakingly and with much love. He said that he just wanted to play. The picture shows a community of houses and a church in the background, and more houses and cars below the train tracks. Bob made many other pictures of community scenes, and most of them included a church. It was at this time that Bob was invited to sing in a boys' choir and there, and at school, he continued to make more friends and to do better in his academic work.

Stages of Development in Sandplay

Bob had moved from the adaptive to the collective, or community stage, rather quickly and did several more scenes of working and playing in a more creative way. Jungians call these stages of development the vegetative, the fighting, and the adapting to the outer or collective life. These stages could just as easily be given psychoanalytical names. The important thing, is to observe the healing process and to be aware of how the individual learns to face his or her gods or archetypes. It is important to make the pain and suffering conscious and to help the individual integrate the split off parts of his or her psyche into a more balanced self.

For Bob, experiencing the archetypal symbols consciously was a necessity in order to rebuild his own psyche. Since he was abandoned as a baby he may have carried the unconscious archetype of abandoned or innocent orphan until he was able to rebuild a stronger ego, and a more centered self. These images and symbols surely have their place in sandplay therapy. Without experiencing them, Bob could have drifted from the victim to victimizer as he had already begun to do at the early age of six. In school he felt he was different because he had been adopted in early childhood. This hindered his development of a real sense of self, especially as he had had no blood mother to separate from creatively. He did however have nourishing adoptive parents and was able to find his own deeper and more satisfying self and center through his sandplay work within a sheltered and sacred place and with a safe friend nearby to guide him. At all times, this therapist kept in close contact with Bob and his parents and received frequent reports from his teachers as well; so she was consciously aware of both his inner and outer world.

Early Infancy and Childhood

In the early stages of Bob's infancy, he was a victim because of the rejection and abandonment of his blood parents. Information is scarce about his birth parents; so it is not known whether or not his mother was at all conscious of her own good and bad mother image. She did make it clear, however, that she did not want to keep her child. Bob must have felt some unconscious rejection and abandonment at an early age. My perception was (after knowing the adoptive parents well) that the adoptive mother was somewhat overbalanced on the side of the good mother archetype, and although this was very helpful to Bob, it might have been better had she been more in touch with, or conscious of, her more human mother. It seemed to me that the father gave a very good example of archetypal spirit to his son, but he too could have set more loving limits when Bob was still quite young.

Summary

To summarize the main stages of development in Bob's therapy, it can be repeated that he was born a victim, perhaps because of archetypal fate. However, with the support of his adoptive parents and the deep archetypal sandplay therapy, he was able to transform his fate into a more creative life. He did start school with a fairly well-organized psyche, but probably not with a clear separation from *bad and good* mother. His earliest images could have been of a bad rejecting mother. Both psychoanalysts and analysts are more aware now that babies desperately need this early identification with mother in order to be able to separate more readily from a loving mother later, in order for a healthy ego and self to develop. Bob needed to rebuild and strengthen his early disorganized ego through therapy plus the loving care of supportive parents. He did suffer much pain in early childhood but learned to accept and understand his fate later and to move into a more balanced and creative living as he developed into early adulthood. His case work surely supports the hypothesis of this study: that humanizing the archetypes leads to healing.

Added Note: As of this date, (March, 1994) Bob is now twenty-seven years of age, has finished high school and college, and is doing well in business.

CASE STUDY #5 - MARY

Woman - Adult - Intergenerational Aspects of Victim

This case study is related to show an example of passive or possessed victim. von Franz (1973) stated that there was a special archetype that impresses its image so deeply on the personality that the individual is possessed. Henderson (1967) agrees with this concept and amplifies it in more detail.

This case study of Mary begins with an account of her mother, Kate, who seemingly was overpowered by an unconscious collective archetype and was forced to live a long period of her life possessed by this image. The case study is mainly about some of the effects on Mary, daughter of Kate, who was the therapist's patient for a period of two years. She had already been in analytical analysis several years before coming to this therapist and appeared to be quite centered and psychically healthy when she first arrived at my office. Mary stated that her reason for seeking further help was that recently, with her oldest brother's death, a sudden surge of archetypal anger that she was unable to cope with, had overtaken her.

In addition, Mary added that her brother's children, who had never been close to her or her sons before, were now showing their aunt much outer hostility and blaming her for upsetting their father just before his death. At this point, it seemed necessary for me to know the full secret that had been in this family for about one hundred years; a secret covering Kate's adult life, her children's lives, part of the lives of her grandchildren, and recently, even some of the events in the lives of the great-grandchildren and other descendants of this unfortunate woman, Kate.

Kate's Story as Remembered by her Daughter Mary

The story of Kate, trapped in victimization, is indeed long and sad. Strangely, Mary had not related any of the past history of her mother to her first therapist. She said that she herself had felt unconsciously victimized for having had to carry the burden of her mother's illness and desertion for the entire family for such a long period of time. Now, with her brother's death, and the secret out in the open, it seemed cruel to have the second generation children blame her, without recognizing some of their own father's responsibility in the sacrifice of his mother.

In spite of Mary's obvious anger, frustration, and sadness, this therapist felt that, although Mary was distraught, her ego was stable and strong and ready to break some of the archetypal influences that she had inherited from her mother's unconsciously lived life. Mary was encouraged to tell the long secret story as clearly as she understood all the facts. This is the story in as brief a form as possible from such a complicated and painful account.

Mary was separated from her mother at a very early age and was unable to see her again until she was an adult. She was told that her mother was dead. The father, older brother, and sister had decided it was best to tell this lie for the protection and good of all concerned. The truth, that Kate had been hospitalized for mental illness, and the four children taken from her and moved many miles away, was just too harsh for this family to admit openly.

At a very early age, Mary had vowed she would some day find her mother and rescue her from her horrible fate. As she looked back on her life in many therapy sessions, she said that she was able to realize that she had lived much of her childhood in planning ways of rescuing her mother. As soon as Mary was old enough to write letters, she contacted relatives and then her mother directly. This secret was kept from her family members. Mary thought that it was because of her great need to be loved that she had kept her loyalty to the family lie.

Nevertheless, Mary said she never forgot her vow to help her mother and did manage to visit her as soon as she had enough money saved to do so. Her true dream, she admitted, was not only to rescue her mother but to bring her back to all the family. Her mother's brother, however, persuaded her against this decision, saying it was too late and that Kate would be miserable in a new place where even her own family rejected her. So Mary came back to her home, married, and had two children before seeing her mother again.

Eight years later, after her mother's brother had died suddenly and there was no one left to take a deep interest in Kate's welfare, Mary returned for another visit. On this occasion, she spent much time in the hospital where Kate was still confined. She talked to the psychiatrists, nurses, and patients. All of the hospital personnel agreed that Kate would be better off outside of the hospital and in a loving home if at all possible. So Mary arranged with a sister-in-law of Kate's to have the two older women live together, as they both were alone now.

Fortunately, Kate had enough money from an inheritance to take care of both of them financially. Several of Mary's cousins lived close by and promised to come to see the two women several times a week. So it was a happy arrangement, and Kate lived out the rest of her life with this sister-in-law. Mary felt that her mother lived her later years in peace, if not in true happiness. My client brought her own children back to see their grandmother several times, and these were happy occasions for all of them, she related. Kate showed the grandchildren love, but sometimes seemed confused between them and her own beloved youngest son, who had actually died in a private airplane crash at the age of 30. At times she knew he was dead but mostly did not want to believe this. The hospital staff had earlier verified that Kate's chief problems arose when she lost contact with reality, temporarily wandering about searching for her baby boy, and refusing to eat.

Mary said she often tried hard to get her mother to express some anger for the way her husband had treated her, but all Kate would ever say was that he did what he thought was best for the children and that he did no wrong. This way, she was able to remain the victim and put all blame on herself. She never seemed to become victimizer except on herself. Mary felt that instead of suffering conscious creative pain, her mother must have lived a dark unconscious life most of her adult life.

Questions Raised in Later Therapy

It is time to return to Mary when she first came to me for therapy. She was fifty years of age; her children were young adults; her mother had died peacefully at age ninety, and her oldest brother had just died, having only quite recently divulged to his own family the story of his mother's life. His account was told in his own way and apparently very differently from the one Mary had known and lived with. It was natural for his children to believe the story as he told it, which, no doubt, accounted for their hostility towards their aunt and great-aunt. However, their ill treatment of her, when Mary felt she should have been loved and respected for having rescued their grandmother and great-grandmother, was too much to bear and brought her in to therapy once more. Mary began to be conscious of the fact that she, too, was being victimized to a degree by the same family that had victimized Kate.

One of the first difficulties that Mary decided to work with was why she could never betray the family when they actually treated her very badly most of the time. She had always found it difficult to lie; so the opposite side or insistence on absolute truth became an obsession for her in the conscious world. This undoubtedly caused a split in her psyche at an early age. Telling the lie was painful, but protecting the good name of the family was also very important.

Mary did tell a few friends and her husband the truth, and later her children. This of course caused difficulties for them as well, since they feared they might divulge the truth to other members of the family, including the cousins. So they also remained loyal to the lie that had caused so much pain for Mary and her children. All of them, especially Mary, adapted to a kind of archetypal-imagery style of family relationships. Without a nourishing mother, Mary felt she attached to an unconscious archetype mother at a very early age; so as an adult, she mothered everything and everyone in a too-possessive manner. Her children suffered from this over-possessive kind of love, she felt, and were able to tell her as adults that it had hindered them in their adjustment to the natural hardships of life.

Mary struggled with other important questions. Why did her mother have to suffer so? Did she have a choice? Or was she just too ill or fragile to live heroically? Or did the gods just hand out her fate and then laugh? Kate had grown up in a wealthy and loving family, so Mary wondered if her mother had just taken the wrong path and married the wrong man? She surely never learned to live successfully in the system and was no doubt engulfed by it and continued to sacrifice her own weak ego.

The main work for Mary in therapy was to become more conscious of how she had been affected by her mother's fate, and what parts of her mother's unconscious victimization she was continuing to carry. Mary was anxious to make whatever pain was still unconscious, conscious so her children could be released from any unconsciously lived part of her own life. At first Mary had felt a great deal of guilt. Had she been born too late in her mother's life, thereby contributing to her ill health? Mostly, Mary felt guilty because she had not been able to stand up to her father, brothers and sister and have them tell the truth and honor their mother. She was caught in the split between familial loyalty, maintaining the lie, and having deeper love for her mother, who so desperately needed support and affection.

Carrying a false hero role proved too heavy a burden for Mary. Unfortunately, part of this unconscious archetype had to be lived out consciously and even later in the lives of her children. Mary finally did realize she had been carrying the load too long, and that she had no doubt related more to the mythic images or archetypes than to her own real and difficult life struggles. She was able to see that, just as her mother had learned only to please, even if it meant sacrificing her own ego, she, too, had tried too hard to please her own family in order to gain their love and affection. She saw, finally, that this was not working and separated more decisively from the *false* family.

The true story about Kate was never revealed by Mary's sister to her husband or children. The children of this family still suffer a great deal, Mary related. However, most of them do talk to Mary and have received much help from their own individual therapy.

Mary's brother's children, though quite brilliant, have suffered deeply from this family lie. Their way to cope was partially through alcohol, drug addiction, and denial. Since they refused to believe the true story of their father and grandmother, Mary has been unable to help them. No doubt it is easier for them to believe their aunt to be wrong rather than to admit that there may be a dark side in the lives of their parents and grandparents.

Mary suffered much from their attitude. She had hoped that, since the secret lie was revealed, the family would be whole again with love and affection among them all. This was an unrealistic dream that may never happen. Mary told this therapist that she had decided to concentrate on her own immediate family, herself, her children, and young grandson.

Method Used in Therapy

Mary's therapy was analytical. She chose to use sandplay, meditation, myth, and active imagination as methods of healing. The main question she worked with regarding her own life was this: "What was she carrying over from her mother's passive victimization? She felt she was not passive and that her fate had followed more the hero role. Even as a young child, she championed her mother's victim role and tried to save her, much like the knights of old with their swords and ideals. She told me she had carried this hero role into her life with her husband and children and later even into the professional world, often standing up for mistreated or neglected individuals.

In meditation and active imagination Mary, was able to become more conscious about her bonding and lack of bonding with her blood mother. She recognized that her mother had not been able to humanize the archetype images that she had been somewhat overcome with from early childhood. Mary was also able to recognize that her mother was not connected to her own deepest being, nor to mother earth, and this kept her from being able to bond consciously. Mary did feel she had bonded to some degree to her mother as a baby and a very young child. She also felt that there had been special love between them when she was young. This made the separation somewhat less painful. Nevertheless, it was still based on archetypal images rather than real life. This image of alliance later became more spiritual and she lived with a deep connection to *the other,* both in her personal and collective life.

Mary knows she was affected by her mother's victimization, but she also feels she was not possessed nor kept from living creatively. Through all the personal hardships of her life—little money, divorce, illnesses, and disappointment—she continued to feel this connection to the *other.* She agreed with this therapist that she may have been a hero victim at times but probably more of the wounded healer as she followed, and began to love, her own fate in life. Her ego was strong, and her struggles seemed to have helped her move closer into consciousness and her own center or self.

Sandplay Therapy Images

Mary produced many sand pictures during her two years of therapy. Four are shown here. In the first picture, she depicts her early archetypal images of her life as a child. It shows a happy family with two children and animals all enclosed in a circle, or mandala, with trees outside the inner circle. It could well represent an actual image of her very early childhood life, or an archetypal wish for a happy family. Other images shown in this study are of the pre-emergence and emergence of Mary's center or self. These images were produced several months later.

Image #1
Mary's Actual or Imagery Childhood Family.

Image #1 shows a happy family encircled by a very simple circle or mandala. Real life seems to be outside the circle and shows a woman riding a horse, dogs, trees, and houses.

Image #2
Pre-Emergence of Self

Image #2 shows the pre-emergence of a center or self. In Mary's case, it is represented by a dancing eagle right in the center of her picture. Community life with dancing figures, houses, people, and animals are shown on the right of the picture and a large Eastern church or mosque on the left back corner. There is an island in the center of the picture, with a large bridge connecting it to the church. This shows unconsciousness and consciousness beginning to connect or become integrated.

Image #3
Emergence of the Self of Center

The last two pictures clearly show the emergence of the Self or center. Image #3 shows the earth goddess, a blue horse, and a white horse in the center of Mary's picture. A larger circle outside this inner one shows the victory goddess, a red horse, a small house, and a Greek windmill style house, which is often referred to as wind or spirit. On the outside four corners of the tray is a large piece of driftwood, a very large house, two other horses, a large fruit tree, a small boy fishing, and two shamanistic birds. This image represents, in classic Jungian terms, an integrated psyche with opposite sides of life clearly depicted.

Image #4
Self-Centered and Amplified

This last picture shows a large stone in the center with a mountain goat standing proudly on top (The Goat is often considered the astrological sign for January, Mary's sign). The center is enclosed with two complete circles of beautiful colored tiles. Two rows of small grey stepping stones lead off to the left and into community life. There is another larger circle outside the smaller ones, like a road, with a princess-like young woman being driven in a Chinese cart. In the righthand back corner, is a beautiful piece of drift wood shaped like a large wooden female person. The entire picture is full of blooming flowers.

Since Mary already had several years of therapy, she had previously worked through most of the elementary stages of development. The last two sand pictures show emergence of self and amplification and verification that she had completed one process of individuation in analytical psychology and was living from her center at this point in her life. She was at a centered place and therapy could be discontinued, at least for the time being.

Effects of Kate's Victimization on
Her Children and Grandchildren

After Mary finished the sandplay pictures she needed to do, she decided to share some events about her sons and other members of the outer family as well, especially those related to Kate's victimization.

She felt that the younger life of her children had been somewhat harsh. Their father deserted when they were young children, and Mary said she had tried unsuccessfully to be both mother and father. Her sons did develop very strong egos and said they never felt they were victims. They struggled with the collective power system but it sounded as though they did live the here and now, and followed their individual fate with love and deep consciousness, somewhat unusual for many young people. Mary brought them to meet and talk with her therapist a few times. They also arranged for some therapy themselves, individually and in groups.

Again, from my knowledge and study of this family, it seems true that they all were affected by some aspects of Kate's victimization, at least at a collective or archetypal level, but none ever became a passive victim. Mary verified that she and her sons remember their mother and grandmother as a very gentle loving person; and though they all express sadness for her fate, they like to think that she has gone on to a different and happier life.

Each member of this family has suffered but also has discovered how to know and to submit positively to both joy and sadness and to love their fate instead of becoming victims to life. Their expressed hope and belief is that the very youngest member, a great-grandson of Kate, will live out his life completely free from the archetypes of victimization, both as passive or possessed victim, and that he will keep a deep consciousness of his own inner child and not become a victimizer. Kate, on the other hand, lived the victim role passively. Although she must have suffered a great deal, it never seemed to be conscious pain. From the account that Mary related, it seems that her strong, early religious beliefs were based more on an innocent desire to see God as a personal heavenly *all good father* rather than as a deep image beyond thought. In addition, she placed her husband in the role of *all good father and husband*, as well, and was unable to confront or face his dark side consciously.

Myth as Healing

Recently, this therapist discovered the following myth. It connects to the story of Mary, and her mother, Kate. That is why it is important to relate it here.

There are many well-known creation myths of gods first being victim in order to create the world. von Franz (1972) tells about many of these, but this particular one is less known. It is an Egyptian myth of a god laughing. He laughed seven times. the first one was for light and fire; the second, for water; and the third, for bitterness. Then with the fourth laugh, Hermes was created for order. On the fifth laugh, god was sad and asked (fate) to help, but she fought with Hermes until justice came from both of them. On the sixth laugh, Cronus came and was given power and light. When god laughed the seventh time, he started to cry so soul and breath were born. Then god bent down to earth and gave birth to a being who gave birth to a dragon and even god was afraid. Thus fear and terror came into the world.

How does this myth relate to Kate? It seems to me, from Mary's story of her family, laughter was simply left out of their life. Maybe Kate just had too weak an ego to face the dragon in laughter; so she became lost in chaos and fear. Perhaps she was unable to truly awaken to the outer world consciously. She certainly had little to laugh joyously about in her early married life of drudgery, with little money and five children to care for. She had been brought up in a wealthy, loving family and was not prepared for such a harsh life with a husband who was unable to show love. Maybe, like Job, she saw God but could not hear him. She faced some terrible events in her life and could not balance or integrate the negative parts or make them conscious. Spontaneous laughter can be a balanced part of creative living.

Summary

When there is a balance of conscious and unconscious, there is an inner experience of ego and Self being connected. Thus the victim role can be transformed and the individual can live out both the fears and the happiness of life. Mary, through pain and submission to her fate and deep therapy in analytical work, made this transition to a more complete experience of Self or center. She did not have to live the victim role, passively. Though she and her children suffered from life's hardships, neither she nor her sons became passively victimized. Each of them experienced victimization many times but were able to contain the pain and move into their true fate.

Mary and her immediate family needed to live out consciously the passive victim role that Kate had been unable to do to its full conclusion. If immortality does continue after life on earth, then, just maybe, Kate will live again a more creative life in a fragment of a star or even in a baby's smile. At least this is Mary's hope and belief for her mother, as expressed to this therapist. In the meantime, she hopes to continue living more consciously and be more related to her family and those individuals who may become a part of her life. I thank her for sharing her moving story with me and giving permission for its contents to be used in this book.

VI. CONCLUSIONS AND FURTHER RESEARCH

This qualitative, Jungian study of victimization and archetype researches a large body of material. The study focuses on phenomenon as it occurs in the context of healing. Four actual sandplay case studies of children and one woman are included. These cases amplify the chief hypothesis of this study: Victimization is a part of the collective unconscious, and thus a part of all individuals. By consciously experiencing and accepting both pain and joy as inevitable, the individual achieves wholeness.

Jung (1939) states that there is no consciousness without a discrimination of opposites. A transcendent function, both conscious and unconscious, occurs from the tension between the opposites that support their union. This transcendent function of the psyche is manifested symbolically in dreams and active imagination.

Active imagination can occur in sandplay in the following way. First, the individual viewing the symbols allows the unconscious to guide him or her in choosing the figures needed for creation. Next, there is a conscious observing of the images—what they mean and how they feel outwardly and inwardly. The symbols chosen can sometimes be related to myths and fairy tales that have meaning for the particular individual.

Creative play is an important part of the process. Victimized children and adults often lose their ability to play and need to relive this lost part of themselves. Active imagination, as generally practiced in Jungian psychotherapy, does not necessarily include play. However, creative play needs to be practiced in all therapies. Fantasies are not just for children.

Active imagination gives voice to parts of the personality that are normally unknown. If taken as an exciting journey into the unconscious, something happens between creator and creation that deepens consciousness. Sometimes painting, writing, or music is used but not necessarily interpreted. The same is true in sandplay; interpretation is not always necessary as long as the therapist is aware and conscious of the process that is happening.

During the process of researching and writing this book, this clinical psychologist has discovered a more balanced way of perceiving victimization through a better understanding of archetypes, which are important in any study of the psyche. When connected to victim the effect of archetypes is discernible through images, for archetypes are attached to nature and the instincts as well.

Jung (1975) states that *the archetype as an image of instinct is a spiritual goal toward which the whole nature of man strives* (par. 415). Archetypes manifest at the personal level as complexes and collectively as characteristics of whole cultures. When one has been victimized, he or she must be willing to submit consciously to the images of archetype both personally and collectively in order for complete healing to take place. This submission is not a surrendering to an evil power. Rather, it means accepting the possibility of transcendence or the union of consciousness and unconsciousness. The ego must participate in both, and this makes transition from one attitude to another possible.

Another way of expressing this is through the term rebirth. Rebirth is a process of renewal or transformation of the personality which cannot be tested or measured. However, it can be experienced and observed in sandplay therapy. The result is a numinous experience for both the therapist and the client. Sometimes, it takes more time for the healing to be evident in the outer or conscious world, but the client is certain that his or her ego is now different. The previous *splitting* of ego is now better understood and the person achieves wholeness. The therapist must first experience his or her own process before being able to help other individuals find healing in either sandplay or active imagination.

Transformation in Sandplay

This author maintains that transformation does occur in sandplay therapy, after the child or adult is able to perceive and experience the deep meaning of the symbols unconsciously produced in his or her own sandplay creations. In this process an unconscious and autonomous movement towards healing manifests itself consciously for the individual. The sandtray creation reveals what is hidden in the unconscious psyche of the victim. In other words, when the victim is finally able to humanize the unconscious archetypes, he or she is no longer possessed and healing takes place.

Qualitative theory does not aim to prove. Instead, it proposes a new theory about the subject being studied. Metaphor is used to make the research more understandable and palatable, especially in clarifying abstract concepts. By understanding metaphor and both the content and images of sandplay therapy and using active imagination, a deeper sense of self emerges within the victim.

It is unproductive to use already published clinical material as examples of the phenomenon addressed in this work, since no specific indices showing victim and archetype as case study were found. This author also used the terms *trauma, sacrifice, masochism, wounded child,* and *scapegoat* to find pertinent research for this study. Differences in *trauma* and *victim,* especially the victim possessed by an archetype, are discussed in other chapters, including Chapter I.

A study of sacrifice traces the history of victim to show how it has been a part of the collective unconscious from the beginning of human history to the present time. This subject is amplified in Chapter IV, which discusses Job, as universal victim. The story of Job as universal victim shows that victimization has been a part of the collective unconscious for a very long time. Several other studies of religious and child sacrifice are reported in this theoretical study. These old accounts relate to Job's story of religious sacrifice and victimization. In addition to the Bible story of Job as victim, there are many more recently published studies about Job's unjust treatment. Some examples are, Meier (1981), Raine

(1982), Edinger (1972), and more recently, Mitchell (1987). Several journal articles on this subject are also reviewed in Chapter III of this work.

Masochism tends more towards death wishes, and not life. The victim may be overwhelmed by circumstances beyond human control, but he or she often continues to fight towards life. The wounded inner child is discussed in detail in this study in Chapters I and II. The child as scapegoat is also covered in other chapters, including Chapters II and V.

Physiological and psychological testing are an important part of case study reporting. However, these areas alone cannot possibly diagnose or treat *soul healing* in the child or adult who is deeply victimized. In addition, published case material lacks the richness and depth of actual clinical case study, especially when this material is chosen from the therapist's own practice. Nevertheless, in case study, it is necessary to focus on the individual as he or she is. The energies and structure of the archetypes have powerful renewal potential, which can open up the healing path. In testing or treating a victimized child or adult, it is important to separate the factors influenced by trauma or emotional effects from actual organic problems. Baxbaum (1983) states that inadequate mothering can lead to mistaken mutism and dissociation until the trauma is cleared. When the emotional factors are separated, cognitive ability can improve in the victimizer as well as in the victim.

The risk factor in divulging the private history of the victimized individual is an important and major concern. Most of the case studies presented here are about people who worked with this therapist a minimum of 15 years prior to this study. This therapist obtained permission to use their material. In addition recent contact was made with each of the participants in this work. One recent child's case study is included because it so clearly exhibits the theory of the victim born to circumstances far beyond his or her control. This therapist honors and appreciates this child's struggle and thanks him and his parents for permission to use his story.

Other Clinical Material

Different types of treatment meet the individual needs of different patients. Among them, sandplay is a sure method of healing. This study and clinical work of other sandplay therapists proves that the patient who has produced a minimum of six to ten sandtray images in a protected environment exhibits more about his or her total self than can be shown through many other diagnostic techniques. (In sandplay therapy, the mother, or father, or sibling is sometimes included in the treatment. The length of treatment depends on the type of family the child or adult is a part of).

What is the root of victimization and why has victimization become epidemic in our modern collective world? This is one of the main questions addressed in this research. Recently, both analysts and psychoanalysts are publishing a great deal of work about reasons for child victimization. These works do not directly mention archetypal victim, but they do add depth to this study. Causes of victimization are often blamed on dysfunctional families, child abandonment, or the loss of parents. Oates (1990) suggests that a loss of parent can be and often is compensated for by an urge to create. He uses Sylvia Plath as example.

Krystal (1978) suggests a somewhat opposite view, stating that every mental illness, when traced to genetic history, can be considered traumatic with a traumatic point of origin. Sandplay therapy looks at trauma and victimization more in terms of finding out what caused the original pain. It focuses on the psyche and the symbols needed for soul-healing. *Psyche* is both the beginning and the end of all understanding. It is the totality of both conscious and unconscious process.

Further research about different kinds of case study is needed to elicit clearer ideas about the changes in the behavior and personality of the victim in treatment. Jungian and Freudian approaches will no doubt continue to differ as long as there is a discrepancy between defining and understanding psychic reality. This divergence, however, should not stop continuing research and the careful use of different methods for healing the victim, especially the borderline victim.

Schwartz-Salant (1989) states that the borderline patient is a person possessed by archetype. The patient, his or her soul ravished in negative affects, is terrified that the therapist will not see his or her suffering. Schwartz-Salant compares this kind of suffering to Job's inner suffering. He also stresses the importance of having faith in the patient and in seeing psychotic mechanisms as something he or she can change with the therapist's support.

Jung (1952), and in many other of his writings, acknowledges that the victim is powerless in the face of being possessed. However, this therapist has witnessed this kind of pain and suffering in many of her clients and has been fortunate enough to observe the transformation that can take place as the archetypes are gradually suffered, made conscious, and finally humanized.

Sandplay therapy as method has not yet been documented, but much research is presently in progress, including dissertations by Miller (1981) and Carmody (1980). Two additional works are in progress at the Center of Psychological Studies and the School of Professional Psychology in Berkeley. One dissertation, De Domenico (1987) and Clegg (1984) are related to sandplay therapy but use a somewhat different method from the Jungian approach

To fully understand the problem of victimization one must realize that the collective unconscious is a structural layer of the human psyche containing inherited elements as well as personal ones. Jung stated that the collective unconscious contains all of our spiritual heritage and is born again in the brain structure of every individual. The more one can become aware of his or her own personal unconscious, the more connected he or she is to the collective.

This realization enlarges one's personality and brings the individual into a better communion with the world at large. When the victim has a conscious and inner knowledge of his or her own center, or self, the petty personal egotistical world of the ego no longer imprisons. This enlargement of personality happens to persons who are willing to understand the larger history and mythology of humankind. In other words, one must accept some responsibility for the unconscious evil within to move the collective forward. This will solve some of the present collective problems including victimization.

The case studies summarized in this work show one method of healing that is possible for the child or adult whose victimization has caused a prior split in personality. The victim's conscious ego is made aware through the process of sandplay therapy and, or, active imagination.

Summary

The subject of victimization covers such a wide field of study that it is difficult to limit what should and should not be included in this work. This study is limited to archetypal victimization in analytical psychology, and to some observations about healing of victim and the victimizer. However, this therapist gained much from reading and researching recent works of psychoanalysts such as Terr (1990), Benjamin (1988), and many object relations authorities such as Winnicott (1964).

This research follows a Jungian, theoretical method. Findings include the following: (1) Archetypal victimization does exist and has from the beginning of time; (2) The victim overcome by archetypes can be healed by experiencing pain and joy consciously. Through working with symbols and active imagination in sandplay therapy, archetypes are finally humanized and healing takes place. Different kinds of healing can take place for both traumatized or victimized individuals through other psychoanalytical and analytical methods of therapy.

This study also discusses the topic of inner and outer child. There is a strong tie between the subject of inner wounded child and some object relation studies. Both nourishing and negative mother have been a part of the collective for a long time. Now these topics are being given more emphasis through in-depth studies. However, the vast topic of imagination is too often forgotten.

This work departs from object relation studies by reaffirming imagination and affirming that victimization is a part of our present collective world. However, victimization studies still need to be perceived at a more critical, imaginative, and deeper level.

Each individual follows in his or her own life the path that humankind has trod before. Each person leaves some trace of the journey in mythological or archetypal images. Archetypes, as patterns of human life, contain healing for humankind. The wounded child must emerge once more as savior or soul archetype, as many post-Jungians are presently predicting.

GLOSSARY

Archetype: According to Jung (1976) archetypes are basic potentialities of imagery and experience. They relate to the collective unconscious. Archetypes include both instinct and spirit. They help to harmonize contrasting opposites such as the Nourishing Mother and the Depriving Mother (rescuer and victim). Edinger, an eminent Jungian scholar, (1965) calls the Self the central archetype; it contains and surrounds all archetypal dominants. There can be dialogue between ego and archetype. Functioning between positive and negative poles, they point to a possible balance for healing.

Collective Unconscious: Jung defines this concept in Collected Works[1]:

> "The collective unconscious is in no sense an obscure corner of the mind, but the mighty deposit of ancestral experience accumulated over millions of years-to be carried on into our own present existence."

He further states that the deposit of world processes is embedded in the brain and nervous system to constitute a totality and eternal world image. He views this as a mirror image to the conscious; the world has an inside and an outside. Although this is part of ancient wisdom, Jung feels that it needs to be evaluated and studied as a new factor in building a new world *(Weltanschauung)*. Edinger amplifies explanations of the collective unconscious:

> "The psyche is not just a product of personal experience. It has also the transpersonal dimensions found in all religions and mythologies. In other words, the collective unconscious comprises the psychic life of our ancestors back to earliest beginnings."

Self: The idea of Self is explained quite clearly by San Francisco Jungian analyst J. Henderson (1990). He sees the Self as the center, a symbol of totality of psychic life, as both circle and the central point within that circle.

"If the circle is the totality, the central point would represent the ordering principle." "It is to be found everywhere; it is the still small voice,"—"a spark of light in the darkness, and its possessor should receive its message in a state of absolute submission" (p. 15).

For further discussion of Self, see Jung (1977) *Collected Works*, Vol 6 p. 460.

Submission: In contrast to the concept of trauma, in which an event is imposed on the subject, the individual sometimes submits sacrificially for the collective good of the society or individual. Usually, submission is thought of as obedience, or the act of being humble. This study uses the word somewhat differently. Although submission means yielding to the power of another, this *other* is actually the Higher Self within our own being. To submit means to connect to God or the gods. The term *submission,* as used in this work, should not be confused with surrendering to or being overwhelmed and completely controlled by another. To submit passively to a victimizer or a more dominant person is very harmful to the ego. However, to ask for help from an omnipotent source is both helpful and healing.

Trauma: The concept of trauma plays a crucial part in the early work of both Freud and Jung, as well as in current psychoanalytical theory and treatment. Both Freud and Jung use the word *trauma,* which is often associated with victim. According to Liliane Frey-Rohn (1974)[2], Jung and Freud agree that the approach to the unconscious should be made by investigating the circumstances that disturb habitual behavior. However, while Freud conceived of the traumatic effects as the primary, precipitating causes of unconscious phenomena, for Jung, the emotion-toned complexes are the central factors in the background of the psyche. Frey-Rhon notes Jung's realization that Freud's explanation of trauma, especially sexual trauma of childhood, was limited. Instead, Jung emphasizes the psychic predisposition of the subject, a factor that determines the effect of the trauma.

Ellenberger (1970) illustrates Jung's method of studying trauma with the case of a 60-year-old patient of Jung's who had spent almost 20 years at Burgholzli clinic. She had abundant hallucinations and delusional ideas that seemed all but incoherent to Jung, who tested her repeatedly with word-association tests, allowing her to free associate to key words about her delusions. In this way, he was able to identify a great number of complexes, which he classifies into three groups: dreams of happiness; complaints of suffering injustices; and sexual complexes. This finding highlights the growing disagreements between Freud and Jung. Freud insists that a traumatic event from the past greatly affects present behavior, while Jung was less interested in looking backwards and more interested in finding the treasure in the future. "Where do we go from here?" he asks. "What is the dream or self trying to do with the complex?"

Post-Jungian literature reveals little direct reference to the word *trauma* or *victim*. Other words, such as *masochism, scapegoat*, and *sacrifice* are used more commonly. Psychoanalysts of the post-Freudian era are more interested in understanding and using the concept of trauma in their practices. The following definitions and explanations of trauma come from earlier works of Freud and Breuer. Lagaache (1957) and Fenichel (1945) define the word *trauma* from a psychoanalytical point of view, as:

> "an event in the subject's life defined by its intensity, by the subjects incapacity to respond adequately to it, and by the upheaval and long-lasting effects that it brings about in the psychical organization. *Trauma* is a term that has long been used in medicine and surgery. It comes from a Greek word meaning wound; it is generally related to an injury caused by external violence. Psychoanalysis carries the three ideas implicit in it over on to the psychical level: the idea of a violent shock, the idea of a wound, and the idea of consequences affecting the whole organization."

Early psychoanalysis related neurosis to past traumatic experiences, proceeding step by step from adulthood back to infancy. Trauma was associated with an event in the subject's personal history. Effective cure came from a psychical working out of the traumatic experiences.

According to Fenichel, some people want to repeat a childhood trauma as a means of abreacting it. The ego desires this repetition to relieve a painful tension; however, the repetition is itself painful. Thus the patient enters a vicious circle, and mastery is never attained. Fenichel feels that these patients illustrate traumatic neuroses and psychoneuroses.

Victim: According to the Oxford Dictionary (1989) *victim* is identified as:

> "a living creature killed and offered as sacrifice to some deity or supernatural power, offered as gift or oblation. It was said that sacrifices of birds and beasts were used as far back as 1613. In the 1700s it was common for victims to be sacrificed to save their nation; many were dragged to the altar in religious rites. In the 1800s the term victim was applied more to Christ as an offering for mankind. Both the priest and the victim (person) were known as 'lambs of sacrifice'. The person was put to death or tortured by another as cruel and oppressive treatment. Victim can relate to the one who perishes or suffers physical distress or one who is badly treated and taken advantage of. In 1975, further use of the word victim was explained as victim hero, slain in sacrifice. Some attributes for victim are: victim beast, carrion, flock, hero, horde, lamb, and victim-laden or victimship."

In earlier times, victim was spelled differently and different terms were used to explain victim and victimizer. Continuing from Oxford:

> "One spelling of the word was *victime*, used universally in the 16th century and by a Rhemish translator of the Bible into English. Besides victime as old spelling, *victimary* was also used as slayer of sacrificial victims by the Romans in 1669; Victimary was used to denote the state of being a victim as late as 1862. In 1893 and later, it was often said that Christ's body was in a Eucharistic state to show the sacrificial

character of the mass. Victimology was said to be a study of victims of crime, with psychological effects rather than causes (a legal term for the sociology of murder)."

It is interesting that as late as 1950, Karen Horney used the term *victimology* in her theory about the treatment of victims. Presently it is being used fairly frequently.

Clinically speaking, she indicates, *victim* can be defined as a living being offered in sacrifice. My definition is no different, as long as the unconscious and conscious split is acknowledged. Victim can be defined as one who finds him or herself at the mercy of another person or of a series of events or misfortunes, such as one who has been molested, abused, or deeply mistreated physically or psychically.

Clearer definitions of Jungian terms can be found in Sharp (1991) and in Jung (1977) *Col.Works* #6. (see references).

Glossary Footnotes

1. Carl Jung, Collected Works, volume VIII (1969).

2. Liliane Frey-Rohn, (1974). *From Freud to Jung: A Comparative Study of the Psychology of the Uncon-scious*, pp. 19-21.

REFERENCES

Abrams, Jeremiah (1990). *Reclaiming the Inner Child*, Jeremy P. Thatcher, Inc., Los Angeles.

Benjamin, Jessica (1988). *The Bonds of Love: Psychoanalysis, Feminism, the Problem of Domination*, Pantheon Books, New York.

Bok, Sissela (1984). Secrets, *On the Ethics of Concealment and Revelation*, Vintage Books (Division of Random House), New York.

Burkhauser-Oeri, Sibylle (1988). *The Mother, Archetypal Image in Fairy Tales*, Inner City Books, Toronto, Canada.

Campbell, Joseph (1988). *The Power of Myth, with Bill Moyers*, Doubleday, New York.

Circlot, J.E. (1982). *Dictionary of Symbols, Second Edition*, Philosophical Library, New York.

Cornes, Tristen (1985). *Melancholia: Archetype of the Divine Victim*, Chiron Press Wilmette, Ill., Cassette Tape.

Cowan, Lynn (1985) *Masochism*, Spring Publications, Dallas.

Davitz, Joel and Lois Jean (1979). *Evaluating Plans in Psychology and Education*, Teachers College Press, New York.

Dickinson, Carolyn Ford, (1989). *George Eliot's Scenes of Clerical Life in Feminine and Myth*, University of Missouri, Columbia.

Dundas, Evalyn T. (1990). *Symbols Come Alive in the Sand*, Coventure Ltd. London, Boston, Mass.

Dundes, Alan (1980). *Interpreting Folklore*, Indiana University Press, New Haven.

Edinger, Edward F. (1972). *Ego and Archetype*, C.G. Jung Foundation for Analytical Psychology, New York.

Elefant-Dietz, Anne Catherine (1981). *The Minotaur in Twentieth Century*, New York University.

Ellenberger, Henri F. (1970). *The Discovery of the Unconscious*, Basic Books, Inc., New York.

Erickson, E.H. (1963). *Childhood and Society*, Second Edition, New York.

Fenichel, O. (1945). *The Psychoanalytic Theory of Neurosis*, W.W. Norton and Company, New York.

Franken, Jos. & Von, Stolk, Bram (1990). *Netherlands Institute for Social Sexological Research*, Utrecht, Netherlands Incest Victims: Inadequate Help by Professionals, Child Abuse and Neglect, Vol. 14 (2) 253-263.

Frankl, Victor, (1969). *Man's Search for Meaning*, Washington Square Press Editions, New York.

Goldenberg, Irene and Herbert (1985). *An Overview of Family Therapy*, Second Edition, Brooks/Cole Publishing Co. Pacific Grove, Ca.

Greene, Robert J. (1981). *Family Therapy, Major Contributions*, James Framo International University. Washington D.C.

Guntrip, Harry (1971). *Psychoanalytic Theory, Therapy, and the Self, A Basic Guide to the Human Personality in Freud, Erikson, Klein, et. al.* Basic Books, Inc., Publishers, New York.

Gunderson, J. (1983). *Personality Disorders*, American Psychology Press, Washington D.C.

Hampsey, John Coleman, (1982). *Blake's Bound Children—A Study of Tiriel and Other Works*, Boston College.

Harrell, Martha Davis (1987). *Women Without Words—Splitting in the Feminine Psyche*, Union For Experimental Colleges/University Without Walls and Union Graduate School.

Henderson, Joseph (1990). *Shadow and Self—Selected Papers in Analytical Psychology*, Chiron Publications, Wilmette, Il.

Henderson, Joseph (1967). *Thresholds of Initiation*, Wesleyan University Press, Middletown, Connecticut.

Horney, Karen *The Neurotic Personality of Our Time*, W.W. Norton and Company, New York.

Jung, C.G. (1976). *The Symbolic Life #18, Collected Works Vols.15-19*, Princeton University Press, Princeton, N.J.

Jung, C.G. (1956). *Symbols of Transformation*, Vol #5, Panatheon Press Inc., New York.

Jung, C.G. (1952). *Answer to Job*, Meridian Books Inc., New York.

Jung, C.G. (1968) *Analytical Psychology, Its Theory and Practice*, Vintage Books, New York.

Jung, C.G. (1977). *Psychological Types*,Vol.#6, Princeton University Press, Princeton New Jersey.

Jung, C.G. (1953). *Psychological Reflections*, Bollingen Foundation Inc. New York.

Jung, C.G. Institute of Los Angeles (1989). "The Child Within/The Child Without. "*Psychological Perspectives*, Issue 21.

Kalff, Dora M. (1971). *Sandplay, Mirror of a Child's Psyche*, Browser Press, San Francisco.

Lagache, D, (1957). *Devie Pathologique La Psychoanalyse*, Paris.

Laing, R.D. and Esterson, A. (1964). *Sanity, Madness and the Family*, Penguin Books Ltd., Harmondsworth, Middlesex, England.

Langs, Robert, (1983). *The Psychotherapeutic Conspiracies*, Jason Aronson Inc., New York.

Matthews, Boris, (1990). *The Herder Symbol Dictionary*, Chiron Publications, Wilmette, Illinois.

Meier, Leui, (1981). *Job, Judiasm and Jung*, Harvest #27

Meyrink, Gustav, (1976). *The Golem*, Dover Publications Inc. New York.

Miller, Alice, (1981). *Prisoners of Childhood*, Basic Books, Inc., New York.

Miller, Alice "Thou Shalt Not Be Aware", an excerpt by Abrams, (1990) from Miller, (p. 189).

Mitchell, Stephen, (1987). *The Book of Job*, North Point Press, San Francisco.

Nagel, Hildegard, *Antwort-An Hiob: Subjective reflections*, Spring, 1954.

Nelson, Thomas, (1952). *The Holy Bible, Revised Standard Version*,New York.

Neumann, Erich (1962). *Amor and Psyche—The Psychic Development of the Feminine*, Harper & Row, New York.

Neumann, Erich (1973). *The Child*, G.P. Putnam's Sons, New York.

Ogden, Thomas (1986). *The Matrix of the Mind, Object Relations*, Northvale, N.J.

Pagels, Elaine (1988). *Adam, Eve, and the Serpent*, Random House, New York.

Pagnucci, Mirta (1981). *The Novels of Grazia, Deledda: Archetypal Structure and Artistic Technique*, University of Wisconsin.

Pearson, Carol (1986). *The Hero Within*, Harper and Row, San Francisco.

Perera, Sylvia (1986). *The Scapegoat Complex*, Inner City Books, Toronto, Canada

Perlman, Michael Ross (1986). *Imaginal Memory: A Study of Psychic Forces Associated with the Place of Hiroshima: A Cross-disciplinary Study in Archetypal Psychology and Religion*, Boston University.

Peroomian, Rubin (1989). *Armenian Literature Responses to Catastrophe Compared with the Jewish Experience*, University of Ca. L.A.

Raine, Kathleen (1982). *The Human Face of God—William Blake and the Book of Job*, Jason Aronson Inc., New York.

Rohn, Lillian Frey (1974). *From Freud to Jung, A Comparative Study of the Psychology of the Unconscious*, G.P. Putnam & Sons, New York,

Ross, Edward N. & Faustini, Richard A. (1990). Escape from Abuse II, *96th Annual Meeting of A.P.A.* (1988). Atlanta, Georgia and Psychotherapy in Private Practice (1990) Vol 8 (1) 119-133.

Samuels, Andrew (1985). *Jung and the Post-Jungians*, Routledge and Kegan, Paul, Boston.

Sharp, Daryl, (1991). *Jung Lexicon*, A Primer of Terms & Concepts, Inner City Books, Toronto, Canada.

Schwartz-Salant, Nathan, (1989). *The Borderline Personality, Vision and Healing*, Chiron Publications, Wilmette, Ill.

Schwartz-Salant, Nathan, (1982). *Narcissism and Character Transformation*, Inner City Books,Toronto, Canada.

Shengold, Leonard (1989). *Soul Murder, The Effects of Childhood Abuse and Deprivation*, Yale University Press, New Haven and London.

Stein, Murray, & Schwartz-Salant, Nathan (1987). *Archetypal Processes In Psychotherapy*, Chiron Publications, Wilmette, Il.

Stern, Daniel (1985). *The Interpersonal World of the Infant*, Basic Books, New York.

Stewart, Harold, (1990). "Interpretation For Psychic Change", *The International Review of Psychoanalysis*, Vol. 17, part I, II, and III, London.

TePaske, Bradley (1982). *Rape and Ritual, A Psychological Study*, Inner City Books Publishing Co., Toronto, Canada.

Terr, Lenore (1990). *Too Scared to Cry, Psychic Trauma in Childhood*, Harper and Row Publishers, New York, San Francisco.

Tuttman, Samuel, Kaye, Carl, and Zimmerman, Muriel (1981-82). *Object and Self, A Developmental Approach;* Also *Essays in Honor of Edith*, Jacobson, International Universities Press, Inc. New York.

Untermeyer, Louis (1968). *Giants of World Literature, Anthology of Wm. Shakespeare*, McGraw Hill Books, Copyright Amaldo Mondadori, New York.

Yin, Robert K. (1989). *Case Study Research, Design and Methods*, Sage Publications, Inc., Newbury Park, Ca.

Vaz, Laura & Kanekar, Suresh (1990). "Predicted and Recommended Behavior of a Woman as a Function of Her Inferred Helplessness in the Dowry and Wife Beating Predicaments." *Journal of Applied Social Psychology*, Vol. 20 (pt2), pp. 751-770.

von Franz, Marie Louise (1972). *Creation Myths*, Spring Publications, Zurich, Switzerland.

von Franz, Marie Louise (1973). Lecture, C. J. Jung Institute, Zurich, Switzerland.

Wallerstein, Robert (1990). "Forty-Two Lives in Treatment: A Study of Psychoanalysis and Psychotherapy." *Journal of San Francisco Jung Institute*, Vol. 9 #4.

Weinrib, Estelle L. (1983). *Images of the Self*, Sigo Press, Boston,Mass.

Winnicott, D.H. (1964). *The Child, The Family and the Outside World*, Penguin Books, Baltimore, Md.

Watkins, Sallie A. (1990) "The Double Victim: The Sexually Abused Child and the Judicial System." *Social Work Journal*, Vol 7 (1)29-42, (Bryce Hospital, Tuscaloosa, Al.)

Magazine Articles

A. Newsweek, (July 24, 1989 and April 30, 1990) *Plight of the Border Orphans* and Vol 113, Jan 2, 1989, *The Cruelest Kind of Grief in Syracuse Compared to Armenia.*

B. Time, (Vol 129-May 11, 1987 p.49) *Sexual Abuse or Abuse of Justice- Man's Fight for Custody.*